Friendship Triangles

By Edyta Sitar *for* *Laundry Basket Quilts*

Landauer Publishing

Acknowledgements

A very special "Thank You" is extended to the many skilled hands and patient minds that have helped me to make this book possible:

- My loving family and friends who support me in everything I do

- Moda Fabrics for the opportunity to design beautiful fabrics that are the starting point for my quilts

- Julie Lillo for adding the special touch to the machine quilting in these projects

- Melinda for creating flower arrangements full of color

- Scott and Curtis from Southern Exposure for welcoming me to their home and gardens where photography was taken

- The Landauer Publishing team for their patience, expertise and seemingly endless hours in bringing this book to life

- All the quilters who have enjoyed my designs over the years and exchanged triangles with me

Copyright © 2009 by Landauer Publishing, LLC
Quilt designs copyright © 2009 by Edyta Sitar

This book was designed, produced, and published by Landauer Publishing, LLC
3100 NW 101st Street, Urbandale, IA 50322
800-557-2144; www.landauercorp.com

President/Publisher: Jeramy Lanigan Landauer
Vice President of Sales & Operations: Kitty Jacobson
Managing Editor: Jeri Simon
Art Director: Laurel Albright
Technical Illustrator: Linda Bender
Technical Editor: Rhonda Matus
Photography: Sue Voegtlin

Library of Congress Control Number: 2009936570

ISBN 13: 978-0-9818040-9-5
ISBN 10: 0-9818040-9-8

This book is printed on acid-free paper.
Printed in China
10 9 8 7 6 5 4 3

Contents

Projects

Triangle Block Exchanges

What's more fun than getting together with other quilters who share your passion for quilting? Whether through shops, guilds, retreats or small groups, being with quilting friends is always special. How about exchanging triangle blocks and fabrics? Get a group of quilting friends together—it doesn't matter if it's two or twenty, if they are new quilters or experienced, everyone is invited to exchange these fun, easy to make triangle blocks.

Triangle Block Exchanges with Friends

Decide on Color—Will your color requirements be the standard light and dark fabrics, or, how about using triangle fabric exchanges to clean out your stash? It's the perfect block exchange for sharing the "What was I thinking about when I bought that" fabric. Or try a color theme—an autumn color palette or reds and pinks to celebrate quilting friends you love.

Use the Same Technique—Everyone should create the blocks using the same technique, thus ensuring each block is consistent. Use a cotton, neutral-color thread when sewing.

Triangle Exchange Paper—We suggest trying the Triangle Exchange Paper, shown here and demonstrated on page 10.

Easy-to-use Triangle Exchange Paper makes (28) 2" finished half-square triangles. When exchanging, do not remove the paper or open the triangles. Opening the triangles and seeing the fabrics will be a fun surprise for your block exchange friends.

Equal Numbers—The number of blocks each quilter receives should equal the number of blocks they have given away. Be sure to keep track of what each quilter gives and receives.

Choose a Project and Begin—Thoughts of special quilting friends will bring a smile as you sew your newest keepsake.

From Edyta—

TRIANGLE BLOCK EXCHANGES IN QUILT SHOPS

It's a wonderful idea for quilt shops to hold triangle block exchanges among customers. Shops holding the block exchanges say the programs are "wildly successful and fun". It's easy to understand why they become a favorite repeat activity for customers.

Half-square triangle blocks can be combined to create beautiful quilts, throws, wallhangings, and table runners. It is even more fun when many different people exchange blocks. Since Quilt Shops have the unique ability to connect with lots of people, holding a triangle block exchange is a great way to bring many quilters together.

Set-up—Have a variety of gorgeous fabrics with Half-Square Triangle Exchange Paper on the counter for customers to buy.

Roll two (2) pieces of 6-1/2" x 21" fabric, one light and one dark, with a sheet of Half-Square Triangle Exchange Paper (2" finished). "I like to call them cinnamon sticks." Set several of these on the counter for customers to purchase. You may want to have a few instructions on the block exchange for them also, as well as a time frame when customers must return the blocks to participate in the exchange.

Instructions—After the customer completes a set of 28 half-square triangles in the same color, they cut them apart and bring them back to the store. The customer's name is added to a list with the number of triangles she has returned.

At the end of the exchange time, each customer will receive a bag of half-square triangle blocks equal to the number of triangles equal she brought to the shop.

Have projects, books, and patterns showing the use of half-square triangles in projects; or offer a class showcasing quilt designs using half-square triangles. You may want to offer a prize recognizing the customer bringing in the most triangles. A block exchange can be done every month to draw in new customers as well those who want to continue.

Edyta Sitar

About the Author...

Edyta Sitar is proud to carry on a family tradition that fabrics and threads have seamlessly stitched together through the generations.

Her true love for quilting and her quilter's spirit shines through in her classes, workshops, and presentations. She travels all over sharing her passion, connecting to and inspiring quilters of all levels by sharing personal and stimulating stories about the quilts she makes.

Quilting has opened a door to another world for Edyta, one in which she can express herself, create beautiful designs, and release her artistic passion. The combination of inspiration from nature, a love for fabric, a keen eye for color, and her family teachings blended into the recipe for developing a flourishing talent for designing quilts, fabrics, and quilting patterns.

"My children and my husband are my greatest motivation, providing the basis that you can accomplish anything you want if you just set your mind to it. Being able to do what I love and share this love with others is the greatest feeling and reward I could imagine! This is the Cinderella dream for me."

As the owner and co-founder of Laundry Basket Quilts, her work has been published in magazines world-wide and her quilts have received numerous awards.

Edyta resides in Marshall, Michigan with her husband and children where she enjoys creating beautiful patterns for Laundry Basket Quilts and designing splendid fabrics for MODA.

Half-Square Triangles

When a project calls for many half-square triangles or I am exchanging triangles with friends the Triangle Exchange Paper makes the process of creating them quick and easy.

Supplies—Laundry Basket Quilts Half Square Triangle Exchange Paper, cotton thread (I prefer Aurifil™ 2370 for color; it blends beautifully with any fabric), acrylic ruler, rotary cutter, cutting mat, pins, and desired light and dark fabric

Cut a 6-1/2" x 21" rectangle from each of the light and dark fabric pieces. Place the light fabric rectangle on the dark fabric rectangle, right sides together.

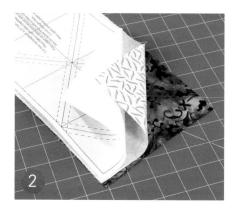

Lay the Triangle Exchange Paper, with printed lines facing up, on top of the light fabric piece. Each sheet of Triangle Exchange Paper will make 28 half-square triangles.

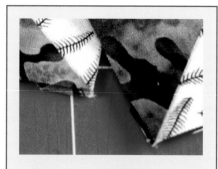

Here's a Tip
The half-square triangle's seam allowance will automatically go toward the dark fabric when the exchange paper is placed on the light fabric.

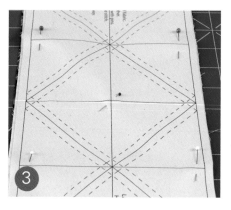

Pin the paper in place using a hopscotch pattern—two pins in the outside triangle markings and one pin in the center. Do not pin over the dashed lines. You will be sewing on these lines.

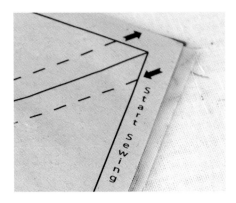

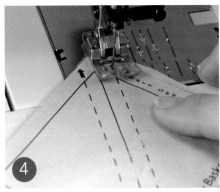

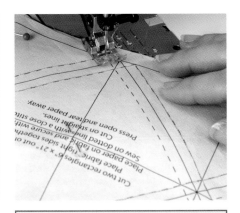

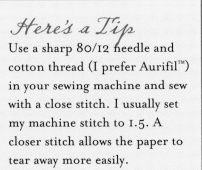

Here's a Tip

Use a sharp 80/12 needle and cotton thread (I prefer Aurifil™) in your sewing machine and sew with a close stitch. I usually set my machine stitch to 1.5. A closer stitch allows the paper to tear away more easily.

Place the corner of the paper marked "Start Sewing" under your presser foot and begin sewing on the dashed line. Sew until you reach the end of the first continuous dashed line.

Here's a Tip

Use the needle down function on your machine while sewing through the paper and fabric. It will allow you to turn the corners without shifting the paper and fabric

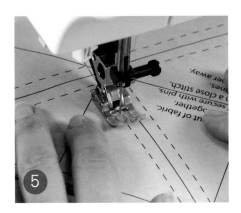

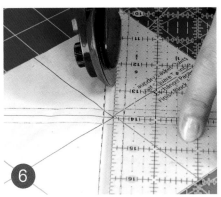

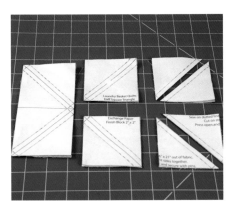

Turn the paper and fabric and follow the arrow to sew the remaining dashed line. Remove the pins.

Using a rotary cutter and acrylic ruler, cut on the solid lines of the Triangle Exchange Paper.

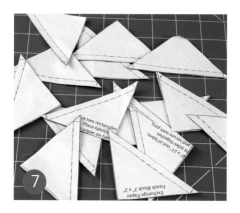

Each sheet of Triangle Exchange Paper will make 28 half-square triangles.

Here's a Tip

If you are exchanging the half-square triangles with friends or through your quilt shop, do not remove the paper or press the triangles open. It makes a fun surprise for the exchange participants to open the triangles they have received.

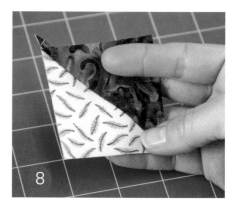

With the paper still attached, press the half-square triangle blocks open. The seam allowance should go toward the darker fabric. Trim the "bunny ears" from the block.

Perforate the Triangle Exchange Paper by pinching the center of the light fabric triangle and the paper.

Remove the paper by tearing from the center to the outside edges of the block.

Your triangles are now ready to be used in any of your favorite projects.

13

Medallion Quilt

Cut the Fabrics

From assorted light to medium prints and batiks, cut:
210—2-7/8" squares
15—4-1/8" squares, cutting each diagonally in an X for a total of 60 setting triangles

From assorted dark prints and batiks, cut:
210—2-7/8" squares

From green batik, cut:
7—1-3/4" x 42" inner border strips

From red batik, cut:
7—1-1/4" x 42" middle border strips
6—2-1/2" x 42" binding strips

From red print, cut:
8—6-1/2" x 42" outer border strips

From backing, cut:
2—33" x 65" rectangles

Assemble the Quilt Center

1. With right sides together, layer a light or medium print or batik 2-7/8" square with a dark print or batik 2-7/8" square. Draw a diagonal line across the wrong side of the light or medium print or batik square.

2. Sew 1/4" on both sides of the drawn line. Cut apart on the drawn line. Press seam toward the dark triangle. The half-square triangles should measure 2-1/2" square.

Repeat Steps 1 and 2 to make a total of 420 half-square triangles.

Make 420 half-square triangles

3. Sew together one half-square triangle and one light to medium print or batik setting triangle for the first row as shown; press.

 Row 1

4. For the second through fourteenth row sew together half-square triangles and a light to medium print or batik setting triangle, increasing the number of half-square triangles by one for each row. The second row has two half-square triangles, the third row three, and so on, ending with 14 in the fourteenth row. Press row seams in one direction, alternating the direction from row to row.

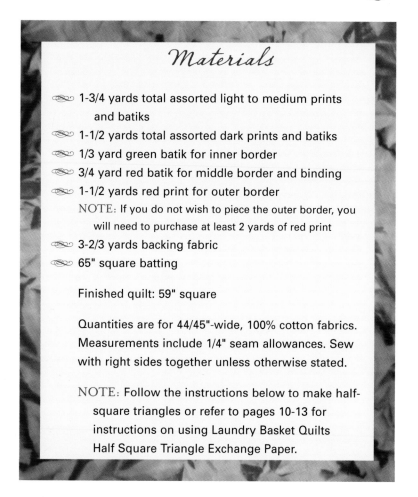

Row 1
Row 2
Row 3
Row 4
Row 5
Row 6
Row 7
Row 8
Row 9
Row 10
Row 11
Row 12
Row 13
Row 14

5. Sew rows 1 to 14 together. Press seams in one direction. Add a light to medium print or batik setting triangle to the first row as shown to complete one large triangle unit.

6. Repeat Steps 3-5 to make a total of four large triangle units.

7. Sew the large triangle units together in pairs. Press seams in opposite directions. Join the pairs together to complete the quilt center.

Add the Borders

1. Piece the green batik 1-3/4" x 42" border strips to make four 1-3/4" x 65" inner border strips.

2. Piece the red batik 1-1/4" x 42" border strips to make four 1-1/2" x 65" middle border strips.

3. Piece the red print 6-1/2" x 42" border strips to make four 6-1/2" x 65" outer border strips.

4. Sew together a green batik inner border strip, a red batik middle border strip, and a red print outer border strip to make a border unit. Press seams toward the outer border. Repeat to make a total of four border units.

Make 4 border units

5. Center and sew a border unit to one edge of the quilt center,

beginning and ending the seam 1/4" from the corners of the quilt center. Press seams toward the border unit. Attach a border unit to each edge of the quilt center in the same manner.

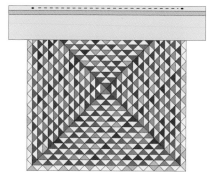

6. Place quilt top right side up on your ironing board. Working with one corner at a time, extend the border unit ends out so the vertical strip overlaps the horizontal strip.

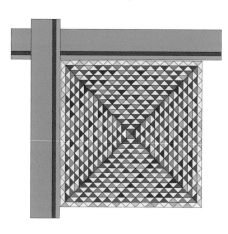

7. Line up the vertical strip and fold it under itself at a 45-degree angle. Check the angle with a ruler and press.

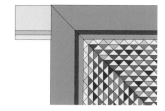

8. With right sides together, fold the quilt on the diagonal so the edges of the two border units line up. Pin and sew along the creased line from the inner point where the previous stitching ends to the outer edge of the border, backstitching to secure. Trim seam to 1/4". Press seam allowance open.

9. Repeat Steps 6-8 for remaining corners.

Complete the Quilt

1. Sew together the 33" x 65" backing rectangles along one long edge, using a 1/2" seam allowance. Press the seam allowance open.

2. Layer quilt top, batting, and pieced backing.

3. Quilt as desired. The Medallion quilt was stitched using a swirl pattern over the entire quilt top.

4. Bind with red batik binding strips.

Here's a Tip

If you have several half-square triangles in one colorway, position them to the outside of the quilt. The blocks will create an invisible border on your project. The Medallion Quilt was pieced with red half-square triangles around the outside edge of the quilt.

Medallion Quilt
Designed and pieced by Edyta Sitar for Laundry Basket Quilts

Ice Cream Sundaes Wallhanging

Materials

- 1/2 yard total assorted light prints and batiks for blocks
- 1/4 yard total assorted dark prints and batiks for blocks
- 3/4 yard dark batik for setting triangles, setting squares and binding
- 5/8 yard gold print for setting triangles
- 32" x 41" backing fabric
- 32" x 41" batting

Finished block: 6" square
Finished table runner: 26" x 34-1/2"

Quantities are for 44/45"-wide, 100% cotton fabrics. Measurements include 1/4" seam allowances. Sew with right sides together unless otherwise stated.

NOTE: Follow the instructions below to make half-square triangles or refer to pages 10-13 for instructions on using Laundry Basket Quilts Half Square Triangle Exchange Paper.

Cut the Fabrics

From assorted light prints and batiks, cut:
28—2-7/8" squares
22—2-1/2" x 4-1/2" rectangles
From assorted dark prints and batiks, cut:
28—2-7/8" squares
From dark batik, cut:
3—9-3/4" squares, cutting each diagonally in an X for a total of 12 setting triangles
2—6-1/2"setting squares
3—2-1/2" x 42" binding strips
From gold print, cut:
5—9-3/4" squares, cutting each diagonally in an X for a total of 20 setting triangles

Assemble the Blocks

1. With right sides together, layer a light print or batik 2-7/8" square with a dark print or batik 2-7/8" square. Draw a diagonal line across the wrong side of the light print or batik square.

2. Sew 1/4" on both sides of the drawn line. Cut apart on the drawn line. Press seam toward the dark triangle. The half-square triangles should measure 2-1/2" square. Repeat Steps 1 and 2 to make a total of 56 half-square triangles.

Make 56
half-square triangles

3. Lay out two matching half-square triangles, three additional half-square triangles, and two light print or batik 2-1/2" x 4-1/2" rectangles with the matching half-square triangles touching as shown.

4. Sew together four half-square triangles in pairs. Press seams in opposite directions. Then join the pairs. Press seam in one direction. Add a light print or batik 2-1/2" x 4-1/2" rectangle to the left edge to complete top section. Press seam toward rectangle.

5. Sew together the remaining light print or batik 2-1/2" x 4-1/2" rectangle and half-square triangle for bottom section. Press seam toward rectangle.

6. Sew together the top and bottom sections to complete one basket block. Press seam toward bottom section.

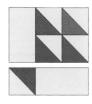

7. Repeat steps 3-6 to make a total of 11 basket blocks. There will be 1 unused half-square triangle.

Assemble the Rows

1. Sew a dark batik setting triangle and a gold print setting triangle to opposite edges of a block to make an A unit as shown. Press seams toward the setting triangles. Repeat to make four A units.

Make 4 A Units

2. Carefully matching seams, sew together the four A units in a row. Press seams in one direction. Add a dark batik setting triangle to the top end and a gold print setting triangle to the bottom end to make Row A.

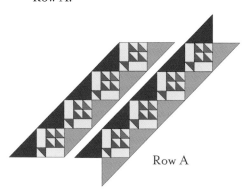

Row A

3. Sew gold print setting triangles to opposite edges of a block to make a B unit as shown. Press seams toward the setting triangles. Repeat to make three B units.

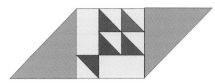

Make 3 B Units

4. Sew a gold print setting triangle to each dark batik 6-1/2" setting square to make a Square-Triangle unit. Press seams toward setting triangles.

Make 2

5. Join the three B units in a row, carefully matching seams. Press seams in one direction. Add a Square-Triangle unit to each end to make Row B. Press seams toward the Square-Triangle units.

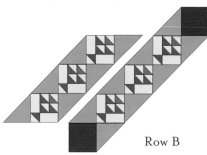

Row B

6. Sew a gold print setting triangle and a dark batik setting triangle to opposite edges of a block to make a

C unit as shown. Press seams toward the setting triangles. Repeat to make four C units.

Make 4 C Units

7. Carefully matching seams, sew together the four C units in a row. Press seams in one direction. Add a gold print setting triangle to the top end and a dark batik setting triangle to the bottom end to make Row C.

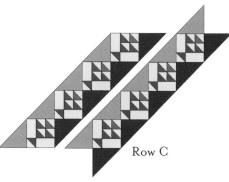

Row C

8. Referring to Wallhanging Assembly Diagram, lay out Row A, B, and C. Join rows to complete wall hanging top. Press seams in one direction.
Note: Trim the wallhanging top after it has been quilted to prevent distortion.

Wallhanging Assembly Diagram

20

Complete the Wallhanging

1. Layer wallhanging top, batting, and backing.

2. Quilt as desired. The wallhanging is stitched with an all-over vine pattern.

3. Trim the wallhanging 1/4" beyond points of blocks in A and C rows.

4. Bind with dark batik binding strips.

Ice Cream Sundaes Wallhanging

Designed and pieced by Edyta Sitar for Laundry Basket Quilts

Mosaic Quilt

Materials

- 1-5/8 yards total assorted dark prints for half-square triangles
- 1-5/8 yards total assorted light or medium prints for half-square triangles
- 2 yards tan-on-tan print for Block 1
- 2 yards tan-and-black print for Block 2 and border
- 5/8 yard dark print for binding
- 5 yards backing fabric
- 75" x 90" batting

Finished blocks: 8" square
Finished quilt: 68-1/2" x 84-1/2"

Quantities are for 44/45"-wide, 100% cotton fabrics. Measurements include 1/4" seam allowances. Sew with right sides together unless otherwise stated.

NOTE: Follow the instructions below to make half-square triangles or refer to pages 10-13 for instructions on using Laundry Basket Quilts Half Square Triangle Exchange Paper.

Cut the Fabrics

From assorted dark prints, cut:
254—2-7/8" squares
From assorted light to medium prints, cut:
254—2-7/8" squares
From tan-on-tan print, cut:
62—2-1/2" x 8-1/2" strips
62—2-1/2" x 4-1/2" strips
From tan-and-black print, cut:
32—4-1/2" squares
7—6-1/2" x 42" border strips
From dark print, cut:
8—2-1/2" x42" binding strips
From backing, cut:
2—38" x 90" rectangles

Making Half-Square Triangles

1. With right sides together, layer a dark print 2-7/8" square with a medium or light print 2-7/8" square. Draw a diagonal line across the wrong side of the medium or light print square.

2. Sew 1/4" on both sides of the drawn line. Cut apart on the drawn line. Press seam toward the dark triangle.

The half-square triangles should measure 2-1/2" square. Repeat Steps 1 and 2 to make a total of 508 half-square triangles.

Make 508
half-square triangles

Assemble Block 1

1. For one Block 1 you will need four half-square triangles, two tan-on-tan print 2-1/2" x 4-1/2" rectangles, and two tan-on-tan print 2-1/2" x 8-1/2" rectangles.

2. Assemble the half-square triangles as shown to make a pinwheel unit. Press seams in a clockwise direction.

3. Sew tan-on-tan print 2-1/2" x 4-1/2" rectangles to the top and bottom edges of the pinwheel unit. Press seams away from the pinwheel unit.

4. Sew tan-on-tan print 2-1/2" x 8-1/2" rectangles to the side edges of the pinwheel unit. Press seams away from the pinwheel unit to complete one Block 1.

5. Repeat Steps 1-4 to make a total of thirty-one Block 1.

Block 1

Assemble Block 2

1. For one Block 2 you will need 12 half-square triangles and one tan-and-black print 4-1/2" square.

2. Sew together four half-square triangles in pairs. Press seams toward dark triangle. Add these to the top and bottom edges of the tan-and-black print 4-1/2" square as shown. Press seams toward the square.

3. Sew together two rows of four half-square triangles as shown. Press seams toward dark triangles.

4. Join the rows to the side edges of the square to complete one Block 2. Press seams toward the square.

5. Repeat Steps 1-4 to make a total of thirty-two Block 2.

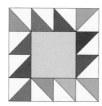

Block 2

Assemble the Quilt Top

1. Referring to Quilt Top Assembly Diagram, lay out thirty-one Block 1 and thirty-two Block 2 in nine horizontal rows.

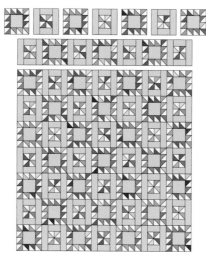

Quilt Top Assembly Diagram

2. Sew together pieces in each row. Press seams in one direction, alternating the direction from row to row. Sew the rows together; press.

3. Piece the tan-and-black print 6-1/2" x 42" border strips to make the following:
2—6-1/2" x 56-1/2" for top and bottom
2— 6-1/2" x 84-1/2" for sides

4. Add the top and bottom border strips to the quilt top. Press the seams toward the border. Add the side border strips to the quilt top. Press the seams toward the border.

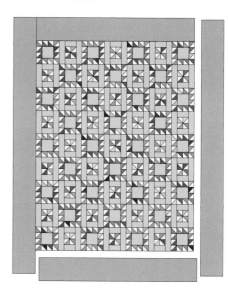

Complete the Quilt

1. Sew together the 38" x 90" backing rectangles along one long edge, using a 1/2" seam allowance. Press the seam allowance open.

2. Layer quilt top, batting, and pieced backing.

3. Quilt as desired. The Mosaic Quilt has a stippling stitch over the entire quilt top.

4. Bind with dark print binding strips.

Mosaic Quilt

Designed and pieced by Edyta Sitar for Laundry Basket Quilts

Tree of Life Wallhanging

Materials

- 3/4 yard total assorted light to medium prints and batiks for blocks
- 3/4 yard total assorted dark prints and batiks for blocks
- 8–9" x 22" (fat-eighths) or 1/8 yard pieces of assorted dark prints and batiks for trunks
- 1 yard off-white batik for blocks
- 1 yard off-white print for setting triangles and corner triangles
- 1/2 yard blue print for binding
- 1/3 yard total assorted green prints and batiks for leaf appliqués
- 6" square blue batik for bird appliqués
- 1/8 yard brown batik for stem appliqués
- Pink print and copper batik scraps for berry appliqués
- 2-5/8 yards backing fabric
- 46" x 66" batting

Finished block: 14" square
Finished quilt: 40" x 59-3/4"
Quantities are for 44/45"-wide, 100% cotton fabrics. Measurements include 1/4" seam allowances. Sew with right sides together unless otherwise stated.

NOTE: Follow the instructions below to make half-square triangles or refer to pages 10-13 for instructions on using Laundry Basket Quilts Half Square Triangle Exchange Paper.

Cut the Fabrics

From assorted light to medium prints and batiks, cut:
72–2-7/8" squares
24–2-1/2" squares

From assorted dark prints and batiks, cut:
72–2-7/8" squares
24–2-7/8" squares, cutting each in half diagonally for a total of 48 A triangles

From each dark print or batik fat-eighths, cut:
1–3-1/4" square, cut diagonally in an X for a total of 4 B triangles
1–4-7/8" square, cut in half diagonally for a total of 2 C triangles
1–3-3/8" x 6-1/8" rectangle

From off-white batik, cut:
2–4-1/2" x 42" strips; use template on page 29 to cut 8 shapes and 8 reversed shapes

4–4-7/8" squares, cutting each in half diagonally for a total o 8 C triangles
8–6-7/8" squares, cutting each in half diagonally for a total of 16 D triangles

From off-white print, cut:
2–21" squares, cutting each diagonally in an X for a total of 8 setting triangles
2–10-3/4" squares, cutting each in half diagonally for a total of 4 corner triangles

From blue print, cut:
5–2-1/2" x 42" binding strips

From backing, cut:
2–33-1/2" x 46" rectangles

Assemble the Blocks

1. With right sides together, layer a light print or batik 2-7/8" square with a dark print or batik 2-7/8" square. Draw a diagonal line across the wrong side of the light print or batik square.

2. Sew 1/4" on both sides of the drawn line. Cut apart on the drawn line. Press seam toward the dark triangle. The half-square triangles should measure 2-1/2" square. Repeat Steps 1 and 2 to make a total of 144 half-square triangles.

Make 144 half-square triangles

3. Lay out six assorted half-square triangles and three light print or batik 2-1/2" squares as shown. Sew the pieces together in rows. Press seams in one direction, alternating

Tree of Life Wallhanging

the direction from row to row. Sew the rows together to complete the top leaf section; press.

4. Lay out six assorted half-square triangles, three dark print or batik A triangles, and one off-white batik D triangle as shown. Sew the half-square triangles and A triangles together in rows. Press seams in one direction, alternating the direction from row to row. Sew the rows together; press. Add the off-white D triangle to complete the right leaf section; press seam toward D.

5. Lay out six assorted half-square triangles, three dark print or batik A triangles, and one off-white batik D triangle as shown. Sew the half-square triangles and A triangles together in rows. Press seams in one direction, alternating the direction from row to row. Sew the rows together; press. Add the off-white D triangle to complete the left leaf section; press seam toward D.

6. Lay out one dark print or batik 3-3/8" x 6-1/8" rectangle, 2 dark print or batik B triangles, one dark print or batik C triangle, one off-white batik C triangle, one template shape, and one template

shape reversed as shown. There will be 2 unused B triangles and one unused C triangle.

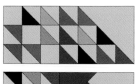

Note: A single dark print or batik was used for the trunk in each of six blocks. The remaining two blocks combined two dark prints for the trunks.

7. Sew a dark print or batik B triangle to the template shaped pieces as shown. Press seams away from the triangles. Sew these to the long edges of the dark print or batik 3-3/8" x 6-1/8" rectangle. Press seams toward rectangle.

8. Add an off-white C triangle to the bottom of the trunk and a dark print or batik C triangle to the top of the trunk to complete one trunk section. Press seams toward C triangle.

9. Sew the top leaf and right leaf sections together for the top half; press seam toward top leaf section. Sew the left leaf and trunk sections together for the bottom half; press seam toward trunk section. Sew the

top and bottom halves together to complete the block. Press seam toward bottom half.

10. Repeat Steps 3-9 to make a total of 8 tree of life blocks.

Assemble the Wallhanging

1. Referring to Wallhanging Assembly Diagram, lay out eight blocks and six off-white print setting triangles in diagonal rows. There will be 2 unused setting triangles.

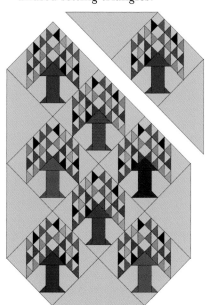

Quilt Top Assembly Diagram

2. Sew together pieces in each row. Press seams in one direction, alternating the direction from row to row.

3. Join rows. Press seams in one direction. Add off-white print corner triangles to complete the wall hanging top. Press seams toward corner triangles.

Appliqué the Wallhanging

1. Trace the appliqué patterns on page 30. Use the appliqué method of your choice to prepare appliqué pieces.

From green prints and batiks, cut:
21 of pattern A (small leaf)
30 of pattern B (middle leaf)
5 of pattern C (large leaf)
5 of pattern C reversed (large leaf reversed)
From blue batik, cut:
1 of pattern D (bird)
1 of pattern D reversed (bird reversed)
From brown batik, cut:
1/4"-wide strips (stems) to make 2-
50" lengths, 6—5" lengths, and
2—3" lengths

From pink print and copper batik, cut:
19 of pattern E (berry)

2. Position the appliqué pieces on the wallhanging top and appliqué the shapes in place using your favorite method.

Complete the Wallhanging

1. Sew together the 33-1/2" x 46" backing rectangles along one long edge, using a 1/2" seam allowance. Press the seam allowance open.

2. Layer quilt top, batting, and pieced backing.

3. Quilt as desired. The wallhanging was quilted using neutral thread, stitched closely around the appliqué shapes and echo-quilted multiple times beyond the shapes. The background and tree-of-life blocks are filled with an all-over wind pattern.

4. Bind with blue print binding strips.

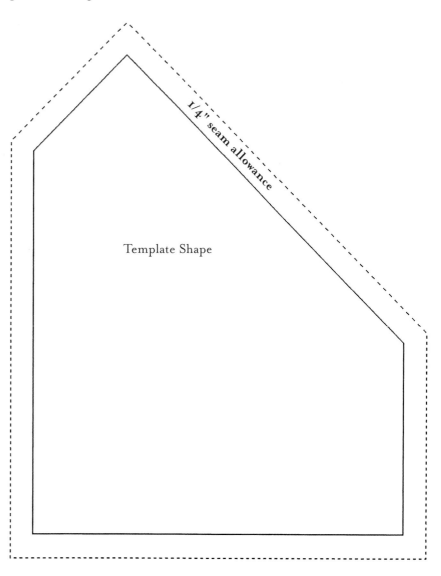

Template Shape

1/4" seam allowance

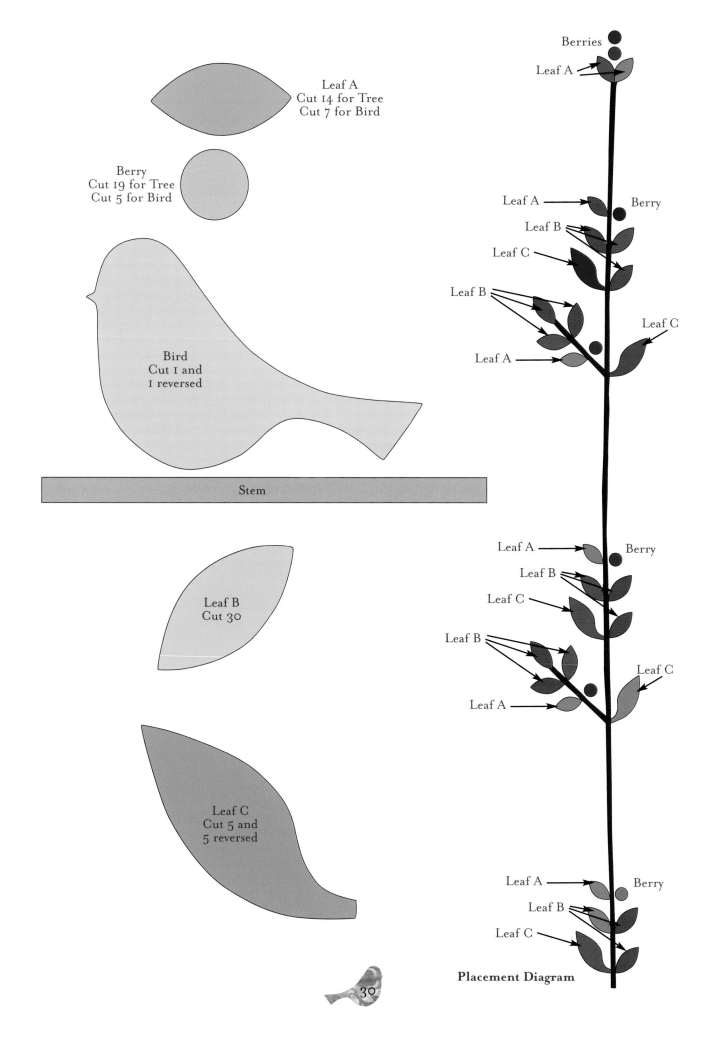

Leaf A
Cut 14 for Tree
Cut 7 for Bird

Berry
Cut 19 for Tree
Cut 5 for Bird

Bird
Cut 1 and
1 reversed

Stem

Leaf B
Cut 30

Leaf C
Cut 5 and
5 reversed

Berries

Leaf A

Leaf A   Berry
Leaf B
Leaf C

Leaf B   Leaf C

Leaf A

Leaf A   Berry
Leaf B
Leaf C

Leaf B   Leaf C

Leaf A

Leaf A   Berry
Leaf B

Leaf C

Placement Diagram

Tree of Life Wallhanging
Designed and pieced by Edyta Sitar for Laundry Basket Quilts

Criss-Cross Quilt

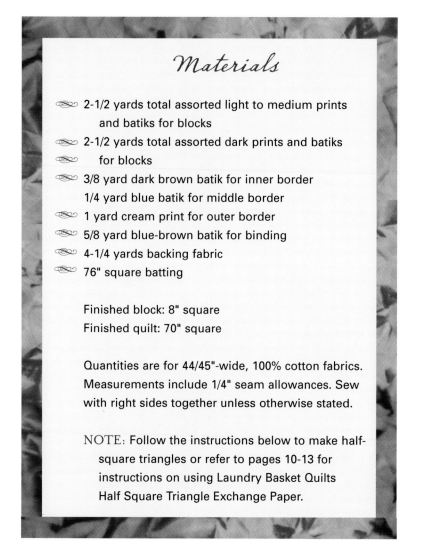

Materials

- 2-1/2 yards total assorted light to medium prints and batiks for blocks
- 2-1/2 yards total assorted dark prints and batiks for blocks
- 3/8 yard dark brown batik for inner border
- 1/4 yard blue batik for middle border
- 1 yard cream print for outer border
- 5/8 yard blue-brown batik for binding
- 4-1/4 yards backing fabric
- 76" square batting

Finished block: 8" square
Finished quilt: 70" square

Quantities are for 44/45"-wide, 100% cotton fabrics. Measurements include 1/4" seam allowances. Sew with right sides together unless otherwise stated.

NOTE: Follow the instructions below to make half-square triangles or refer to pages 10-13 for instructions on using Laundry Basket Quilts Half Square Triangle Exchange Paper.

Cut the Fabrics

From assorted light to medium prints and batiks, cut:
392—2-7/8" squares
From assorted dark prints and batiks, cut:
392—2-7/8" squares
From dark brown batik, cut:
6—2" x 42" inner border strips
From blue batik, cut:
6—1-1/4" x 42" middle border strips
From cream print, cut:
7—5" x 42" outer border strips
From blue-brown batik, cut:
7—2-1/2" x 42" binding strips

From backing, cut:
2—38-1/2" x 76" rectangles

Assemble the Blocks

1. With right sides together, layer a light or medium print or batik 2-7/8" square with a dark print or batik 2-7/8" square. Draw a diagonal line across the wrong side of the light or medium print or batik square.

2. Sew 1/4" on both sides of the drawn line. Cut apart on the drawn line. Press seam toward the dark triangle. The half-square triangles should measure 2-1/2" square. Repeat Steps 1 and 2 to make a total of 784 half-square triangles.

Make 784
half-square triangles

3. Lay out four matching half-square triangles and 12 assorted half-square triangles with the matching half-square triangles at the center of the block as shown.

4. Sew the half-square triangles together in rows. Press seams in one direction, alternating the direction from row to row. Sew the rows together; press. The block measures 8-1/2" square.

5. Repeat Steps 3 and 4 to make a total of 49 blocks. You will use 49 sets of 4 matching half-square triangles (196 half-square triangles) and 588 assorted half-square triangles to make the 49 blocks.

Criss-Cross Quilt

Assemble the Quilt Center

1. Referring to Quilt Center Assembly Diagram lay out 49 blocks in seven horizontal rows, as shown.

2. Sew the blocks in each row together. Press seams in one direction, alternating each row's direction.

3. Join rows to make the quilt center. Press seams in one direction. The quilt center should be 56-1/2" square.

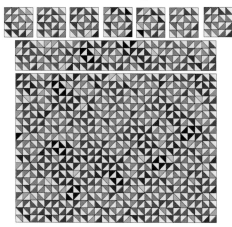

Quilt Center Assembly Diagram

Add the Borders

1. Piece the dark brown batik 2" x 42" inner border strips to make the following:
   2–2" x 56-1/2" for sides
   2– 2" x 59-1/2" for top and bottom

2. Referring to Quilt Top Assembly Diagram, sew the side inner border strips to the quilt center. Press the seams toward the border. Add the top and bottom border strips to the quilt center. Press the seams toward the border.

3. Piece the blue batik 1-1/4" x 42" middle border strips to make the following:
   2– 1-1/4" x 59-1/2" for sides
   2–1-1/4" x 61" for top and bottom

4. Add the side middle border strips to the quilt top. Press the seams toward the middle border. Add the top and bottom middle border strips to the quilt top. Press the seams toward the middle border.

5. Piece the cream print 5" x 42" outer border strips to make the following:
   2– 5" x 61" for sides
   2–5" x 70" for top and bottom

6. Add the side outer border strips to the quilt top. Press the seams toward the outer border. Add the top and bottom outer border strips to the quilt top. Press the seams toward the outer border.

Complete the Quilt

1. Sew together the 38-1/2" x 76" backing rectangles along one long edge, using a 1/2" seam allowance. Press the seam allowance open.

2. Layer quilt top, batting, and pieced backing.

3. Quilt as desired. The quilt was stitched using a stylized leaf pattern over the entire quilt top.

4. Bind with blue-brown batik binding strips.

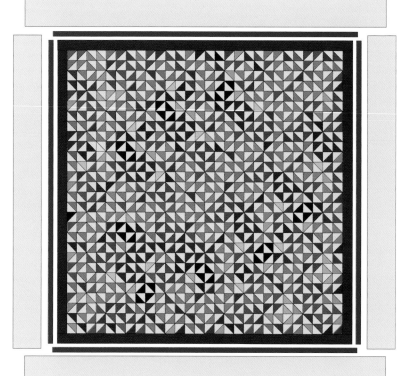

Quilt Top Assembly Diagram

Criss-Cross Quilt

Designed and pieced by Edyta Sitar for Laundry Basket Quilts

Delfina's Basket Quilt

Materials

- 4 yards total assorted light to medium prints for blocks, setting squares, setting triangles and corner triangles
- 1-1/2 yards total assorted dark prints for blocks
- 7/8 yard brown tone-on-tone for inner border and binding
- 1 yard green tone-on-tone for outer border
- Embroidery floss: green and red
- Embroidery needle
- 5 yards backing fabric
- 74" x 88" batting

Finished block: 10" square
Finished quilt: 67-1/2" x 81-1/2"

Quantities are for 44/45"-wide, 100% cotton fabrics. Measurements include 1/4" seam allowances. Sew with right sides together unless otherwise stated.

NOTE: Follow the instructions below to make half-square triangles or refer to pages 10-13 for instructions on using Laundry Basket Quilts Half Square Triangle Exchange Paper.

Cut the Fabrics

Cut the 2-1/2" x 6-1/2" rectangles in sets of two; each block uses two matching light to medium print rectangles.

From assorted light to medium prints, cut:

60—2-7/8" squares

10—8-7/8" squares, cutting each in half diagonally for a total of 20 A triangles

10—4-7/8" squares, cutting each in half diagonally for a total of 20 B triangles

20—2-1/2" x 6-1/2" rectangles

12—10-1/2" setting squares

4—15-1/4" squares, cutting each diagonally in an X for a total of 16 setting triangles

2—7-7/8" squares, cutting each in half diagonally for a total of 4 corner triangles

From assorted dark prints, cut:

60—2-7/8" squares

60—2-7/8" squares, cutting each in half diagonally for a total of 120 C triangles

20—1-1/4" x 12" bias-cut handle strips

From brown tone-on-tone, cut:

7—1-1/4" x 42" inner border strips

8—2-1/2" x 42" binding strips

From green tone-on-tone, cut:

7—4-3/4" x 42" outer border strips

From backing, cut:

2—37-1/2" x 88" rectangles

Assemble the Blocks

1. With right sides together, layer a light or medium print 2-7/8" square with a dark print 2 7/8" square. Draw a diagonal line across the wrong side of the light or medium print square.

2. Sew 1/4" on both sides of the drawn line. Cut apart on the drawn line. Press seam toward the dark triangle. The half-square triangles should measure 2-1/2" square. Repeat Steps 1 and 2 to make a total of 120 half-square triangles.

Make 120 half-square triangles

3. Referring to handle placement diagram on page 39 and diagram below, mark the handle position on a light or medium print A triangle.

4. Fold one dark print 1-1/4" x 12" bias strip in half with wrong sides together; press. Place the strip's cut edges on the marked line with

the fold toward the inside of the curve; pin in place. Sew 1/4" from cut edges.

5. Fold handle over stitching and seam allowance; press lightly. Blind-stitch folded edge of handle to A triangle. Trim strip ends even with triangle.

6. Repeat Steps 3–5 to make a total of 20 appliquéd A triangles.

7. Lay out one appliquéd A triangle, six assorted half-square triangles, and 4 assorted dark print C triangles as shown. Sew the half-square triangles and C triangles together in rows. Press seams in one direction, alternating the direction from row to row. Sew the rows together; press. Add the appliquéd A triangle to complete the basket section; press seam toward A.

8. Sew assorted dark print C triangles to two 2-1/2" x 6-1/2" rectangles for the left and right side sections as shown.

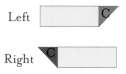

9. Lay out the basket section, the two side sections, and one light or medium print B triangle. Sew the side sections to the basket section. Press seams toward the side sections. Add the B triangle; press seam toward B.

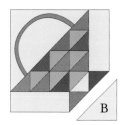

10. Repeat steps 7–9 to make a total of 20 basket-with-handle blocks.

Assemble the Quilt Center

1. Referring to Quilt Center Assembly Diagram, lay out 20 blocks, 12 light or medium print 10-1/2" setting squares, and 14 light or medium print setting triangles in diagonal rows. There will be two unused setting triangles.

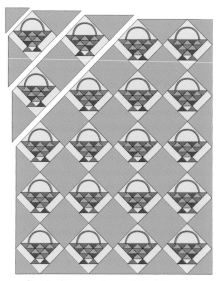

Quilt Center Assembly Diagram

2. Sew the pieces together in rows. Press seams toward the setting pieces.

3. Join rows. Press seams in one direction. Add four corner triangles to complete the quilt center. Press seams toward the corner triangles. The quilt center should measure 57" x 71".

Add the Borders

1. Piece the brown tone-on-tone 1-1/4" x 42" inner border strips to make the following:
   2—1-1/4" x 71" for sides
   2—1-1/4" x 58-1/2" for top and bottom

2. Referring to Quilt Top Assembly Diagram, sew side inner border strips to the quilt center. Press the seams toward the border. Add the top and bottom inner border strips to the quilt center. Press the seams toward the border.

3. Piece the green tone-on-tone 4-3/4" x 42" outer border strips to make the following:
   2—4-3/4" x 72-1/2" for sides
   2—4-3/4" x 67-1/2" for top and bottom

4. Referring to Quilt Top Assembly Diagram, sew side outer border strips to the quilt center. Press the seams toward the border. Add the top and bottom outer border strips to the quilt center. Press the seams toward the border.

Complete the Quilt

1. Referring to page 40, use green floss to backstitch the stem on the bottom left block and the adjacent setting square. Satin-stitch the buds with red floss.

2. Sew together the 37-1/2" x 88" backing rectangles along one long edge, using a 1/2" seam allowance. Press the seam allowance open.

3. Layer quilt top, batting, and pieced backing.

4. Quilt as desired. All the setting squares, setting triangles and corner triangles are stitched in-the-ditch and then filled with stippling.

5. Bind with brown tone-on-tone binding strip

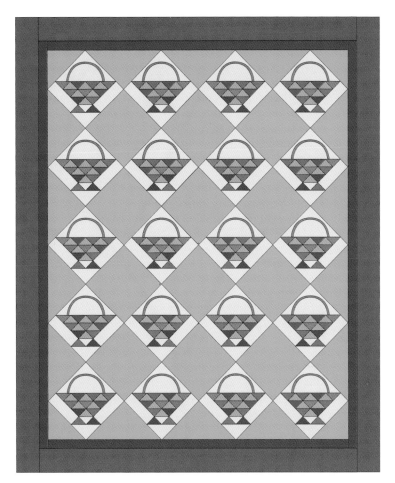

Quilt Top Assembly Diagram

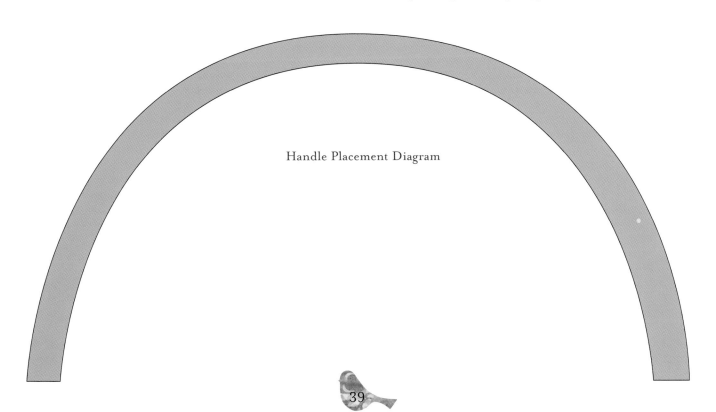

Handle Placement Diagram

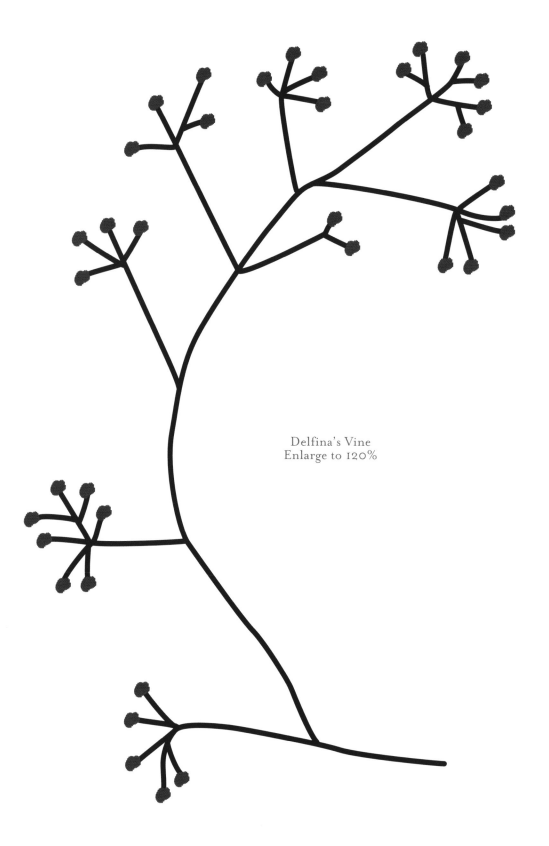

Delfina's Vine
Enlarge to 120%

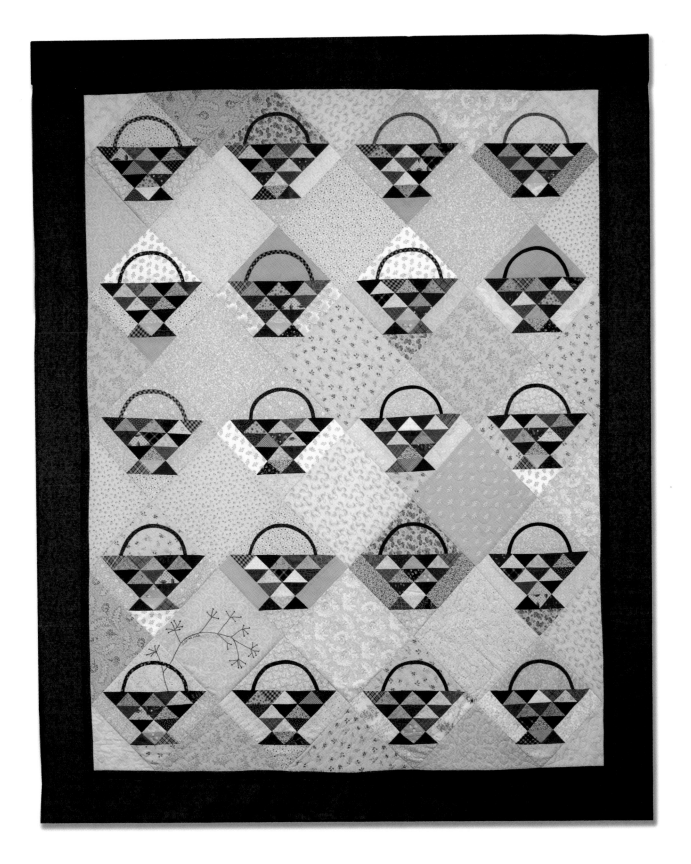

Delfina's Basket Quilt

Designed and pieced by Edyta Sitar for Laundry Basket Quilts

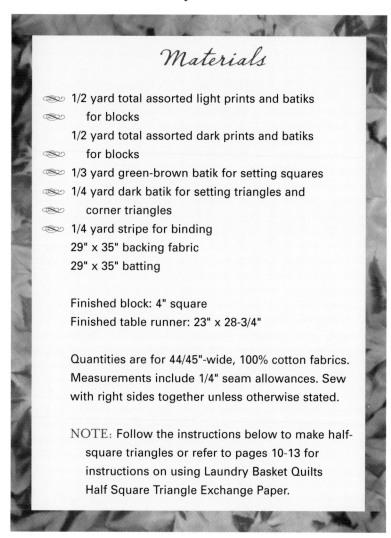

Materials

- 1/2 yard total assorted light prints and batiks for blocks
- 1/2 yard total assorted dark prints and batiks for blocks
- 1/3 yard green-brown batik for setting squares
- 1/4 yard dark batik for setting triangles and corner triangles
- 1/4 yard stripe for binding
  29" x 35" backing fabric
  29" x 35" batting

Finished block: 4" square
Finished table runner: 23" x 28-3/4"

Quantities are for 44/45"-wide, 100% cotton fabrics. Measurements include 1/4" seam allowances. Sew with right sides together unless otherwise stated.

NOTE: Follow the instructions below to make half-square triangles or refer to pages 10-13 for instructions on using Laundry Basket Quilts Half Square Triangle Exchange Paper.

Cut the Fabrics

From assorted light prints and batiks, cut:

20—2-1/2" squares
20—2-7/8" squares

From assorted dark prints and batiks, cut:

20—2-1/2" squares
20—2-7/8" squares

From green-brown batik, cut:

12—4-1/2" setting squares

From dark batik, cut:

4—7" squares, cutting each diagonally in an X for a total of 16 setting triangles

2—3-3/4" squares, cutting each in half diagonally for a total of 4 corner triangles

From stripe, cut:

3—2-1/2" x 42" binding strips

Assemble the Blocks

1. With right sides together, layer a light print or batik 2-7/8" square with a dark print or batik 2-7/8" square. Draw a diagonal line across the wrong side of the light print or batik square.

2. Sew 1/4" on both sides of the drawn line. Cut apart on the drawn line. Press seam toward the dark triangle. The half-square triangles should measure 2-1/2" square. Repeat Steps 1 and 2 to make a total of 40 half-square triangles.

Make 40
half-square triangles

3. Lay out two half-square triangles, one light print or batik 2-1/2" square, and one dark print or batik 2-1/2" square as shown.

4. Sew the pieces together in pairs. Press seams toward the squares. Join pairs to make a triangle-square four-patch block. Repeat Steps 3 and 4 to make a total of 20 triangle-square four-patch blocks.

Make 20

Cabbage Rose Table Runner

Assemble the Table Runner Top

1. Referring to Table Runner Top Assembly Diagram, lay out 20 triangle-square four-patch blocks, 12 green-brown batik setting squares, and 14 dark batik setting triangles in diagonal rows. There will be 2 unused setting triangles.

Table Runner Top Assembly Diagram

2. Sew together pieces in each row. Press seams toward setting pieces.

3. Join rows. Press seams in one direction. Add dark batik corner triangles to complete the table runner top. Press seams toward the corner triangles.

Complete the Table Runner

1. Layer table runner top, batting, and backing.

2. Quilt as desired. The table runner is stitched with an all-over vine pattern.

3. Bind with stripe binding strips.

44

Cabbage Rose Table Runner
Designed and pieced by Edyta Sitar for Laundry Basket Quilts

Materials

- 1 yard total assorted light to medium prints for blocks
- 1 yard total assorted dark prints for blocks
- 1/2 yard motif print for block centers
- 1-1/3 yards green print for setting squares, setting triangles and corner triangles
- 1 yard brown print for border
- 1/2 yard brown-and-tan print for binding
- 3-3/4 yards backing fabric
- 58" x 67" batting

Finished block: 6" square
Finished quilt: 52" x 60-1/2"

Quantities are for 44/45"-wide, 100% cotton fabrics. Measurements include 1/4" seam allowances. Sew with right sides together unless otherwise stated.

NOTE: Extra motif print fabric has been added to allow for fussy-cutting. If you are NOT fussy-cutting you will need 1/4 yard of motif print.

NOTE: Follow the instructions below to make half-square triangles or refer to pages 10-13 for instructions on using Laundry Basket Quilts Half Square Triangle Exchange Paper.

Cut the Fabrics

Cut the 2-7/8" squares in sets of four; each block uses four matching light to medium print squares and four matching dark print squares.

From assorted light to medium prints, cut:

120—2-7/8" squares

From assorted dark prints, cut:

120—2-7/8" squares

From motif print, cut:

30—2-1/2" squares, centering a motif in each square

From green print, cut:

20—6-1/2" squares

5—9-3/4" squares, cutting each diagonally in an X for a total of 20 setting triangles

2—5-1/8" squares, cutting each in half diagonally for a total of 4 corner triangles

From brown print, cut:

6—5" x 42" border strips

From brown-and-tan print, cut:

6—2-1/2" x 42" binding strips

From backing, cut:

2—26-1/2" x 67" rectangles

Assemble the Blocks

1. With right sides together, layer a light or medium print 2-7/8" square with a dark print 2-7/8" square. Draw a diagonal line across the wrong side of the light or medium print square.

2. Sew 1/4" on both sides of the drawn line. Cut apart on the drawn line. Press seam toward the dark triangle. The half-square triangles should measure 2-1/2" square. Repeat Steps 1 and 2 to make a total of 240 half-square triangles.

Make 240 half-square triangles

3. Lay out eight matching half-square triangles and one motif print 2-1/2" square as shown.

4. Sew the pieces together in rows. Press seams in one direction, alternating the direction from row to row. Sew the rows together; press. The block measures 6-1/2" square.

5. Repeat Steps 3 and 4 to make a total of 30 blocks. You will use 30 sets of 8 matching half-square triangles (240 half-square triangles) to make the 30 blocks.

Assemble the Quilt Center

1. Referring to Quilt Center Assembly Diagram lay out 30 blocks, 20 green print 6-1/2" setting squares, and 18 green print setting triangles in diagonal rows, as shown. There will be 2 unused setting triangles. Sew the pieces together in rows. Press seams toward the setting pieces.

2. Join rows. Press seams in one direction. Add green print corner triangles to complete the quilt center. Press seams toward the corner triangles. The quilt center should measure 43" x 51-1/2".

Add the Border

1. Piece the brown print 5" x 42" border strips to make the following:
   2—5" x 51-1/2" for sides
   2—5" x 52" for top and bottom

2. Referring to Quilt Top Assembly Diagram, sew side border strips to the quilt center. Press the seams toward the border. Add the top and bottom border strips to the quilt center. Press the seams toward the border.

Complete the Quilt

1. Sew together the 26-1/2" x 67" backing rectangles along one long edge, using a 1/2" seam allowance. Press the seam allowance open.

2. Layer quilt top, batting, and pieced backing.

3. Quilt as desired. The entire quilt top was stitched using an all-over floral pattern.

4. Bind with brown-and-tan print binding strips.

Quilt Center Assembly Diagram

Quilt Top Assembly Diagram

Album of Friends Quilt
Designed and pieced by Edyta Sitar for Laundry Basket Quilts

Southern Exposure Basket Quilt

Materials

- 1 yard total assorted light to medium prints and batiks for half-square triangles
- 5/8 yards total assorted dark prints and batiks for blocks
- 9—9" x 22" (fat-eighths) pieces of assorted dark prints and batiks for baskets
- 3/4 yard beige batik for block background
- 2-1/4 yards green batik for setting triangles and corner triangles
- 1/2 yard brown print for setting triangles
- 1/2 yard brown-blue batik for binding
- 4-3/8 yards backing fabric
- 63" x 77" batting

Finished block: 10" square
Finished quilt: 57" x 71"

Quantities are for 44/45"-wide, 100% cotton fabrics. Measurements include 1/4" seam allowances. Sew with right sides together unless otherwise stated.

NOTE: Follow the instructions below to make half-square triangles or refer to pages 10-13 for instructions on using Laundry Basket Quilts Half Square Triangle Exchange Paper.

Cut the Fabrics

Note: First cut the 15-1/4" squares from the green batik, and then use the leftover to cut the 7-7/8" squares.

From assorted light to medium prints and batiks, cut:

90—2-7/8" squares

27—2-7/8" squares, cutting each in half diagonally for a total of 54 A triangles

From assorted dark prints and batiks, cut:

90—2-7/8" squares

From each dark print or batik fat-eighth, cut:

2—2-7/8" squares, cutting each in half diagonally for 4 A triangles (36 total)

1—6-7/8" square, cut in half diagonally for 2 B triangles (18 total)

From beige batik, cut:

36—2-1/2" x 6-1/2" rectangles

9—4-7/8" squares, cutting each in half diagonally for a total of 18 C triangles

From green batik, cut:

9—15-1/4" squares, cutting each diagonally in an X for a total of 36 setting triangles

6—7-7/8" squares, cutting each in half diagonally for a total of 12 corner triangles

From brown print, cut:

1—15-1/4" squares, cutting each diagonally in an X for a total of 4 setting triangles

From brown-blue batik, cut:

7—2-1/2" x 42" binding strips

From backing, cut:

2—32" x 77" rectangles

Assemble the Blocks

Note: Each basket is made using a single dark print or batik for two half-square triangles, two A triangles, and the B triangle. Position the matching half-square triangles in opposite corners of the basket section touching the matching B triangle.

1. With right sides together, layer a light or medium print or batik 2-7/8" square with a dark print or batik 2-7/8" square. Draw a diagonal line across the wrong side of the light or medium print or batik square.

2. Sew 1/4" on both sides of the drawn line. Cut apart on the drawn line. Press seam toward the dark triangle. The half-square triangles should measure 2-1/2" square. Repeat Steps 1 and 2 to make a total of 180 half-square triangles.

Make 180 half-square triangles

3. Lay out 8 assorted half-square triangles, two matching half-square triangles, three light or medium print or batik A triangles, and one dark print or batik B triangle as shown. Sew the half-square triangles and A triangles together in rows. Press seams in one direction, alternating the direction from row to row. Sew the rows together; press. Add the B triangle to complete the basket section; press seam toward B.

4. Sew matching dark print or batik A triangles to two beige batik 2-1/2" x 6-1/2" rectangles for the left and right side sections as shown.

5. Lay out the basket section, the two side sections, and one beige batik C triangle. Sew the side sections to the basket section. Press seams toward the side sections. Add the C triangle; press seam toward C.

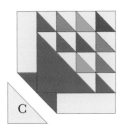

6. Repeat steps 3-5 to make a total of 18 blocks.

Assemble the Quilt Top

1. Sew green batik setting triangles to opposite edges of a block to make a Block-Triangle unit as shown. Press seams toward the setting triangles. Repeat to make a total of 12 Block-Triangle units.

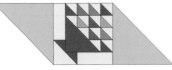

Make 12

2. Sew a green batik setting triangle and a green batik corner triangle to opposite edges of six blocks, making three of each Corner-Triangle unit as shown.

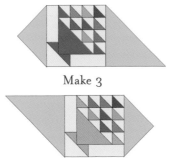

Make 3

Make 3

3. Sew together a brown print setting triangle and a green batik setting triangle to make a Triangle Pair unit as shown. Press seams toward green batik setting triangle. Repeat to make a total of four Triangle Pair units. There will be two unused green batik setting triangles.

Make 4

4. Carefully matching seams, sew together two Block-Triangle units and two Corner-Triangle units in a row as shown. Press seams in one

direction. Add a green batik corner triangle to each end to make Row A. Press seams toward the corner triangles. Repeat to make a total of three Row A.

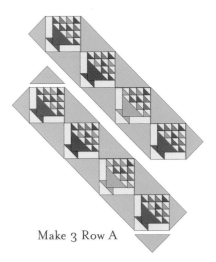

Make 3 Row A

5. Carefully matching seams, sew together three Block-Triangle units and two Triangle Pair units to make Row B. Press seams in one direction. Repeat to make a second Row B.

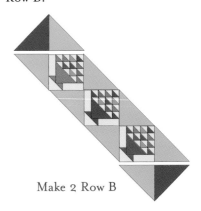

Make 2 Row B

6. Referring to the photograph at right, lay out alternating A and B row. Join rows to complete quilt top. Press seams in one direction.

Complete the Quilt

1. Sew together the 32" x 77" backing rectangles along one long edge, using a 1/2" seam allowance. Press the seam allowance open.

2. Layer quilt top, batting, and pieced backing.

3. Quilt as desired. Each block was stitched in-the-ditch and also along the basket seams. The baskets were filled with a 2" grid and the remaining block areas were filled with stippling. The green batik setting pieces have an all-over swirl pattern and a 3/4" grid was added over the brown print setting squares.

4. Bind with brown-blue batik binding strips.

Southern Exposure Basket Quilt

Designed and pieced by Edyta Sitar for Laundry Basket Quilts

Constellation Throw

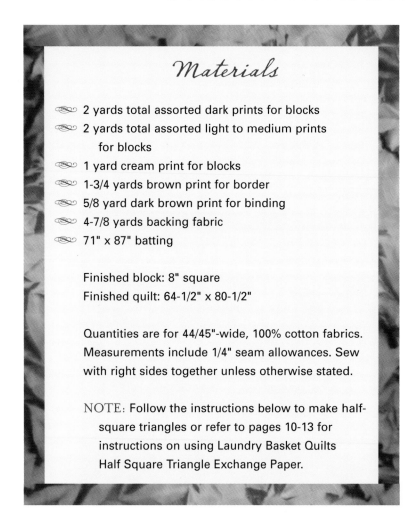

Materials

- 2 yards total assorted dark prints for blocks
- 2 yards total assorted light to medium prints for blocks
- 1 yard cream print for blocks
- 1-3/4 yards brown print for border
- 5/8 yard dark brown print for binding
- 4-7/8 yards backing fabric
- 71" x 87" batting

Finished block: 8" square
Finished quilt: 64-1/2" x 80-1/2"

Quantities are for 44/45"-wide, 100% cotton fabrics. Measurements include 1/4" seam allowances. Sew with right sides together unless otherwise stated.

NOTE: Follow the instructions below to make half-square triangles or refer to pages 10-13 for instructions on using Laundry Basket Quilts Half Square Triangle Exchange Paper.

Cut the Fabrics

From assorted dark prints, cut:
288—2-7/8" squares
From assorted light to medium prints, cut:
288—2-7/8" squares
From cream print, cut:
192—2-1/2" squares
From brown print, cut:
7—8-1/2" x 42" border strips
From dark brown print, cut:
8—2-1/2" x 42" binding strips
From backing fabric, cut:
2—36" x 87" rectangles

Assemble the Blocks

1. With right sides together, layer a light or medium print 2-7/8" square with a dark print 2-7/8" square. Draw a diagonal line across the wrong side of the light or medium print square.

2. Sew 1/4" on both sides of the drawn line. Cut apart on the drawn line. Press seam toward the dark triangle.

The half-square triangles should measure 2-1/2" square. Repeat Steps 1 and 2 to make a total of 576 half-square triangles.

Make 576
half-square triangles

3. For each block you will need 12 half-square triangles and four cream print 2-1/2" squares.

4. Sew four half-square triangles together in pairs. Press seams in opposite directions. Join pairs to make a triangle four-patch unit. Repeat to make a second triangle four-patch unit.

5. Sew two half-square triangles and two cream print 2-1/2" squares together in pairs. Press seams toward the squares. Join pairs to make a triangle-square four-patch unit. Repeat to make a second triangle-square four-patch unit.

6. Lay out two triangle four-patch units and two triangle-square four-patch units as shown. Sew the units together in pairs. Press seams toward the triangle-square four-patch units. Join pairs to

make a Constellation block. Press seams one direction.

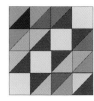

7. Repeat Steps 3–6 to make a total of 48 Constellation blocks.

Assemble the Throw Center

1. Referring to Throw Center Assembly Diagram, lay out 48 blocks in eight horizontal rows.

2. Sew the blocks in each row together. Press seams in one direction, alternating each row's direction.

3. Join rows to make the throw center. Press seams in one direction. The throw center should be 48-1/2" x 64-1/2".

Add the Border

1. Piece the brown print 8-1/2" x 42" border strips to make four 8-1/2" x 64-1/2" border strips.

2. Referring to Throw Top Assembly Diagram, sew border strips to the long edges of the throw center. Press seams toward the border. Add the remaining border strips to the top and bottom edges. Press seams toward the border.

Complete the Throw

1. Sew together the 36" x 87" backing rectangles along one long edge, using a 1/2" seam allowance. Press the seam allowance open.

2. Layer throw top, batting, and pieced backing.

3. Quilt as desired. The throw was stitched using an X pattern over the entire quilt top.

4. Bind with dark brown print binding strips.

Throw Center Assembly Diagram

Throw Top Assembly Diagram

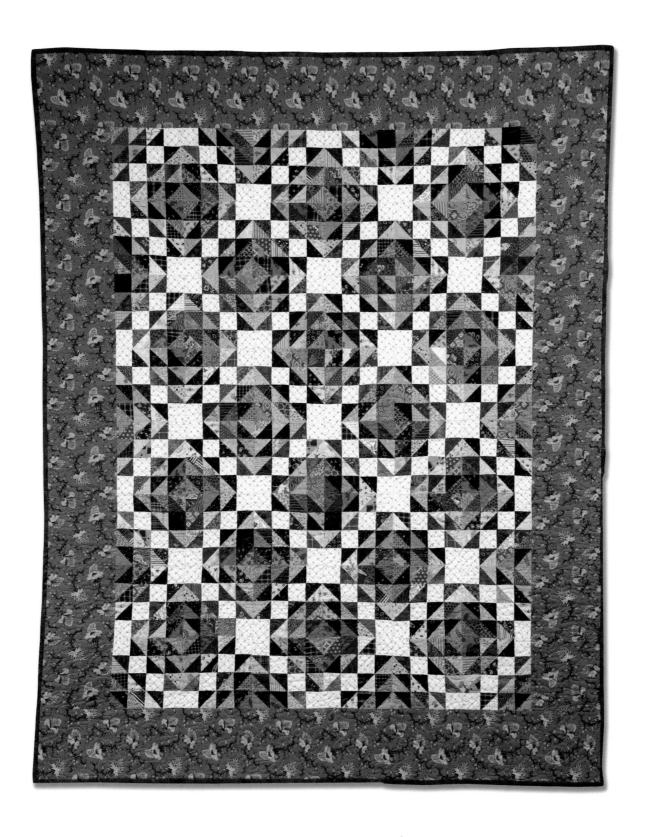

Constellation Throw

Designed and pieced by Edyta Sitar for Laundry Basket Quilts

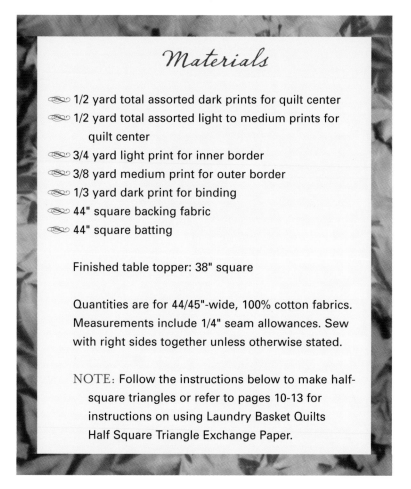

Materials

- 1/2 yard total assorted dark prints for quilt center
- 1/2 yard total assorted light to medium prints for quilt center
- 3/4 yard light print for inner border
- 3/8 yard medium print for outer border
- 1/3 yard dark print for binding
- 44" square backing fabric
- 44" square batting

Finished table topper: 38" square

Quantities are for 44/45"-wide, 100% cotton fabrics. Measurements include 1/4" seam allowances. Sew with right sides together unless otherwise stated.

NOTE: Follow the instructions below to make half-square triangles or refer to pages 10-13 for instructions on using Laundry Basket Quilts Half Square Triangle Exchange Paper.

Cut the Fabrics

From assorted dark prints, cut:
61—2-7/8" squares
From assorted light to medium prints, cut:
61—2-7/8" squares
From light print, cut:
4—5-3/4" x 36" inner border strips
From medium print, cut:
2—3" x 33" outer border strips
2—3" x 38" outer border strips
From dark print, cut:
5—2-1/2" x 42" binding strips

Assemble the Table Topper Center

1. With right sides together, layer a dark print 2-7/8" square with a medium or light print 2-7/8" square. Draw a diagonal line across the wrong side of the medium or light print square.

2. Sew 1/4" on both sides of the drawn line. Cut apart on the drawn line. Press seams toward the dark triangle. The half-square triangles should measure 2-1/2" square. Repeat Steps 1 and 2 to make a total of 122 half-square triangles.

Make 122
half-square triangles

3. Lay out the half-square triangles in eleven rows of eleven half-square triangles as shown. There will be one unused half-square triangle.

4. Sew the half-square triangles together in rows. Press seams in one direction, alternating the direction from row to row. Sew the rows together; press. The topper center measures 22-1/2" square.

Little Pyramids Table Topper

Add the Borders

1. Center and sew a light print 5-3/4" x 36" inner border strip to one edge of the topper center, beginning and ending the seam 1/4" from the corners of the topper center. Attach an inner border strip to each edge of the topper center in the same manner. Press seams toward the border.

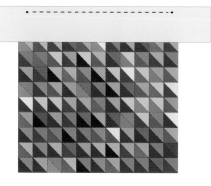

2. Place table topper right side up on your ironing board. Working with one corner at a time, extend the border ends out so the vertical strip overlaps the horizontal strip.

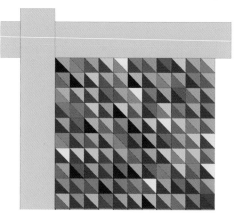

3. Lift up the vertical strip and fold it under itself at a 45-degree angle. Check the angle with a ruler and press.

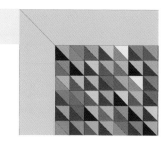

4. With right sides together, fold the table topper on the diagonal so the edges of the two border strips line up. Pin and sew along the creased line from the inner point where the previous stitching ends to the outer edge of the border, backstitching to secure. Trim seam to 1/4". Press seam allowance open.

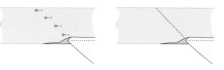

5. Repeat Steps 2–4 for remaining corners.

6. Referring to the Table Topper Assembly Diagram, sew medium print 3" x 33" outer border strips to opposite edges of the topper. Press seams toward outer border. Add medium print 3" x 38" outer border strips to remaining edges. Press seams toward outer border.

Complete the Quilt

1. Layer quilt top, batting, and backing.

2. Quilt as desired. The table topper center is filled with meandering pattern and an X motif in the borders.

3. Bind with dark print binding strips.

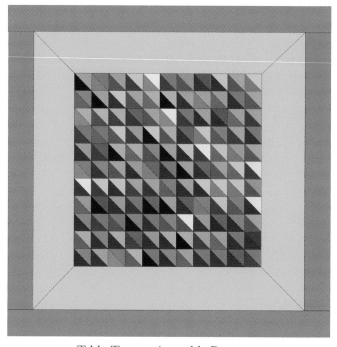

Table Topper Assembly Diagram

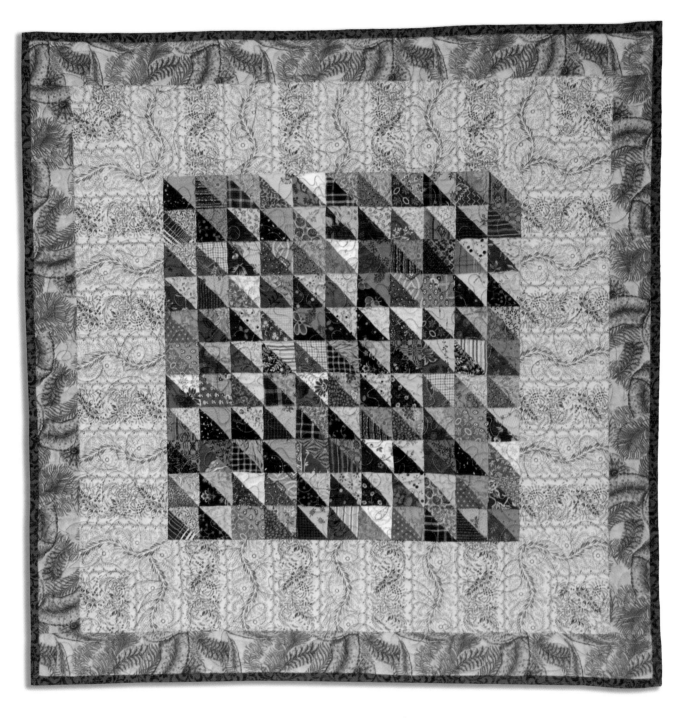

Little Pyramids Table Topper

Designed and pieced by Edyta Sitar for Laundry Basket Quilts

Garden Path Quilt

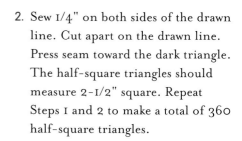

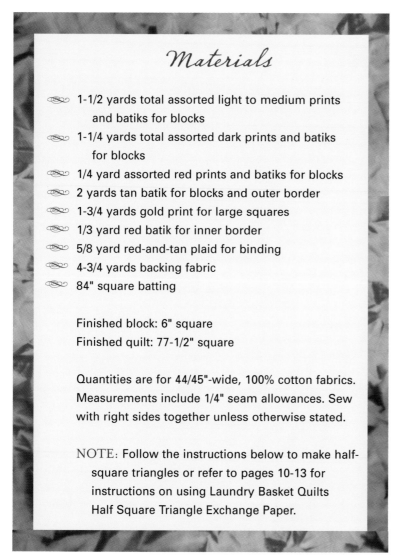

Materials

- 1-1/2 yards total assorted light to medium prints and batiks for blocks
- 1-1/4 yards total assorted dark prints and batiks for blocks
- 1/4 yard assorted red prints and batiks for blocks
- 2 yards tan batik for blocks and outer border
- 1-3/4 yards gold print for large squares
- 1/3 yard red batik for inner border
- 5/8 yard red-and-tan plaid for binding
- 4-3/4 yards backing fabric
- 84" square batting

Finished block: 6" square
Finished quilt: 77-1/2" square

Quantities are for 44/45"-wide, 100% cotton fabrics. Measurements include 1/4" seam allowances. Sew with right sides together unless otherwise stated.

NOTE: Follow the instructions below to make half-square triangles or refer to pages 10-13 for instructions on using Laundry Basket Quilts Half Square Triangle Exchange Paper.

Cut the Fabrics

From assorted light to medium prints and batiks, cut:
180—2-7/8" squares
60—2-1/2" squares
From assorted dark prints and batiks, cut:
180—2-7/8" squares
From assorted red prints and batiks, cut:
48—2-1/2" squares
From tan batik, cut:
60—2-1/2" x 6-1/2" rectangles
8—5" x 42" outer border strips
From gold print, cut:
49—6-1/2" squares
From red batik, cut:
8—1-1/2" x 42" inner border strips

From red-and-tan plaid, cut:
8—2-1/2" x 42" binding strips
From backing, cut:
2—42-1/2" x 84" rectangles

Assemble Block 1

1. With right sides together, layer a light or medium print 2-7/8" square with a dark print 2-7/8" square. Draw a diagonal line across the wrong side of the light or medium print square.

2. Sew 1/4" on both sides of the drawn line. Cut apart on the drawn line. Press seam toward the dark triangle. The half-square triangles should measure 2-1/2" square. Repeat Steps 1 and 2 to make a total of 360 half-square triangles.

Make 360 half-square triangles

3. Sew together six half-square triangles in two rows of three as shown. Press seams toward dark triangles.

4. Lay out the two half-square triangle rows and one tan batik 2-1/2" x 6-1/2" rectangle as shown. Sew rows and rectangle together to complete one block. Press seams toward rectangle. The block measures 6-1/2" square.

5. Repeat Steps 3 and 4 to make a total of 60 Block 1.

Assemble Block 2

1. Lay out five light print or batik 2-1/2" squares and four red print or batik 2-1/2" squares as shown.

2. Sew the squares together in rows. Press seams toward light squares. Sew the rows together to complete one block; press. The block measures 6-1/2" square.

Note: The seams in Block 2 are pressed in the opposite direction of the seams in Block 1. This will aid in setting the blocks together in rows.

3. Repeat Steps 1 and 2 to make a total of 12 Block 2.

Assemble the Quilt Center

1. Referring to Quilt Center Assembly Diagram, lay out 60 Block 1, 12 Block 2, and 49 gold print 6-1/2" squares in eleven horizontal rows, as shown.

2. Sew the pieces together in rows. Press seams away from Block 1. Sew the rows together; press. The quilt center should measure 66-1/2" square.

Add the Borders

1. Sew together the red batik 1-1/2" x 42" border strips in pairs to make four inner border strips.

2. Sew together the tan batik 5" x 42" border strips in pairs to make four outer border strips.

3. Sew together a red batik inner border strip and a tan batik outer border strip to make a border unit. Press seam toward the outer border. Repeat to make a total of four border units.

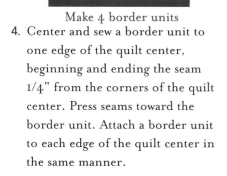

Make 4 border units

4. Center and sew a border unit to one edge of the quilt center, beginning and ending the seam 1/4" from the corners of the quilt center. Press seams toward the border unit. Attach a border unit to each edge of the quilt center in the same manner.

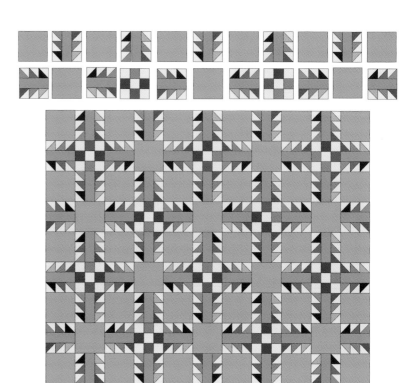

Quilt Center Assembly Diagram

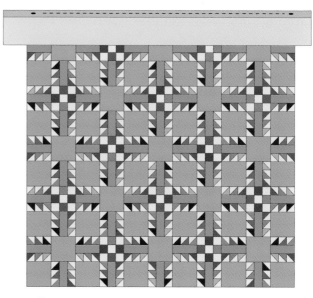

5. Place quilt top right side up on your ironing board. Working with one corner at a time, extend the border unit ends out so the vertical strip overlaps the horizontal strip.

6. Line up the vertical strip and fold it under itself at a 45-degree angle. Check the angle with a ruler and press.

7. With right sides together, fold the quilt on the diagonal so the edges of the two border units line up. Pin and sew along the creased line from the inner point where the previous stitching ends to the outer edge of the border, backstitching to secure. Trim seam to 1/4". Press seam allowance open.

8. Repeat Steps 5-7 for remaining corners.

Complete the Quilt

1. Sew together the 42-1/2" x 82" backing rectangles along one long edge, using a 1/2" seam allowance. Press the seam allowance open.

2. Layer quilt top, batting, and pieced backing.

3. Quilt as desired. The Garden Path quilt was stitched using a vine pattern over the entire quilt top.

4. Bind with red-and-tan plaid binding strips.

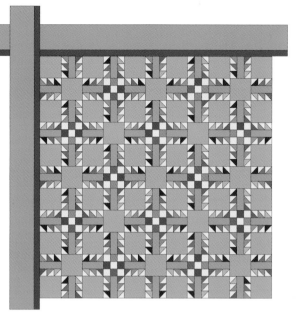

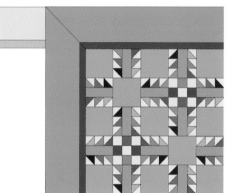

Fold vertical strip at a 45-degree angle

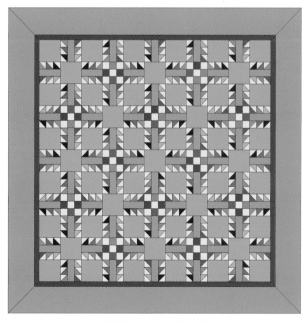

Quilt Top Assembly Diagram

Garden Path Quilt

Designed and pieced by Edyta Sitar for Laundry Basket Quilts

Tote Bag

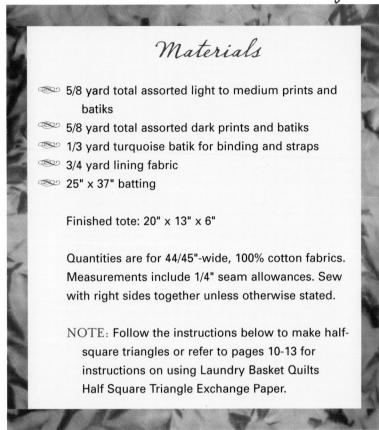

Materials

- 5/8 yard total assorted light to medium prints and batiks
- 5/8 yard total assorted dark prints and batiks
- 1/3 yard turquoise batik for binding and straps
- 3/4 yard lining fabric
- 25" x 37" batting

Finished tote: 20" x 13" x 6"

Quantities are for 44/45"-wide, 100% cotton fabrics. Measurements include 1/4" seam allowances. Sew with right sides together unless otherwise stated.

NOTE: Follow the instructions below to make half-square triangles or refer to pages 10-13 for instructions on using Laundry Basket Quilts Half Square Triangle Exchange Paper.

Cut the Fabrics

From assorted light to medium prints and batiks, cut:
80—2-7/8" squares
From assorted dark prints and batiks, cut:
80—2-7/8" squares
From turquoise batik, cut:
1—2-1/4" x 42" binding strip
2—4" x 24" strap strips
From lining, cut:
1—25" x 37" rectangle
2—2-1/2" x 18" lining strips

Assemble the Tote Front

1. With right sides together, layer a light to medium print or batik 2-7/8" square with a dark print or batik 2-7/8" square. Draw a diagonal line across the wrong side of the light or medium print square.

2. Sew 1/4" on both sides of the drawn line. Cut apart on the drawn line. Press seam toward the dark triangle. The half-square triangles should measure 2-1/2" square. Repeat Steps 1-2 to make a total of 160 half-square triangles.

Make 160 half-square triangles

3. Sew together 10 half-square triangles to make 1 row as shown. Press seams toward dark triangles.

The row should measure 2-1/2" x 20-1/2". Repeat to make a total of 16 rows.

4. Sew the rows together in pairs as shown. Press seams in one direction.

5. Sew the pairs together to complete the tote front. Press seams in one direction. The tote front should measure 20-1/2" x 32-1/2".

Complete the Tote Bag

1. Layer pieced tote front, batting, and lining.

2. Quilt as desired. The tote was quilted with neutral thread and a stippling stitch. Trim the batting and lining even with edges of tote front.

3. With pieced sides together, fold quilted tote rectangle in half to measure 20-1/2" x 16-1/4". Using a 1/4" seam, sew the 16-1/4" edges together for the left and right sides of the bag. Bind side seams with 2-1/2" x 18" lining strips, folding under bottom ends of strips and catching in hand-stitching.

4. To box bottom of bag, work with the bag inside out and align one side seam with the center bottom of the bag. Measure 3" from the point and sew through all layers. Repeat for remaining side of bag.

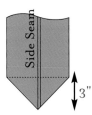

5. With right sides together, fold a turquoise batik 4" x 24" strap strip in half and sew long edges together. Turn strap right side out and press, centering the seam on one side of the strap. Repeat for second strap.

6. Pin the strap ends on the lining side of the bag 4-3/4" from the side seams, aligning the ends with the top edge of the bag. Sew ends in place. Repeat for remaining strap on opposite side of bag.

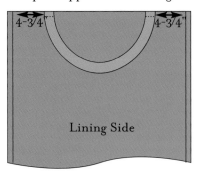

7. Bind the top edge of bag with turquoise batik binding strip, enclosing the strap ends in binding.

Book Cover

Materials

- 1/4 yard total assorted light to medium prints and batiks
- 1/4 yard total assorted dark prints and batiks
- 1/8 yard turquoise batik for binding and ties
- 1/2 yard lining fabric
- 21" x 15" batting
-
- Finished book cover: 16-1/2" x 10-1/2"

Quantities are for 44/45"-wide, 100% cotton fabrics. Measurements include 1/4" seam allowances. Sew with right sides together unless otherwise stated.

NOTE: Follow the instructions below to make half-square triangles or refer to pages 10-13 for instructions on using Laundry Basket Quilts Half Square Triangle Exchange Paper.

Cut the Fabrics

From assorted light to medium prints and batiks, cut:
20—2-7/8" squares
From assorted dark prints and batiks, cut:
20—2-7/8" squares
From turquoise batik, cut:
2—2-1/4" x 42" binding strip
2—2" x 9-1/2" tie strips
From lining, cut:
1—21" x 15" rectangle
2—12-1/2" x 10-1/2" inside pocket rectangles

Book Cover

Assemble the Book Cover Front

1. With right sides together, layer a light to medium print or batik 2-7/8" square with a dark print or batik 2-7/8" square. Draw a diagonal line across the wrong side of the light or medium print square.

2. Sew 1/4" on both sides of the drawn line. Cut apart on the drawn line. Press seam toward the dark triangle. The half-square triangles should measure 2-1/2" square. Repeat Steps 1-2 to make a total of 40 half-square triangles.

Make 40 half-square triangles

3. Sew together 8 half-square triangles to make 1 row as shown. The row should measure 2-1/2" x 16-1/2". Repeat to make a total of 5 rows. Press seams in one direction, alternating the direction from row to row.

4. Sew the rows together to complete the book cover front. Press seams in one direction. The book cover front should measure 16-1/2" x 10-1/2".

Complete the Book Cover

1. Layer pieced book cover front, batting, and 21" x 15" lining rectangle.

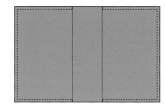

2. Quilt as desired. The book cover was quilted with neutral thread and a stippling stitch. Trim the batting and lining even with edges of book cover front.

3. Press under 1/2" on the long edges of a turquoise batik 2" x 9-1/2" tie strip. Fold strip in half lengthwise, aligning the pressed edges; press again. Sew the long edges together opposite the fold. Repeat for second tie.

4. On the pieced side of the cover, sew a tie centered on each short edge.

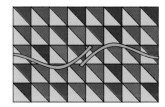

5. With wrong sides together, fold each 12-1/2" x 10-1/2" inside pocket rectangle in half to measure 6-1/4" x 10-1/2"; press.

6. On the lining side of cover, position an inside pocket at one short edge of the cover with pressed edge toward the center of the cover. Baste pocket in place along top, side, and bottom edges of cover. Repeat for second pocket at the remaining short edge of cover.

7. Bind all edges of cover with turquoise batik binding strips.

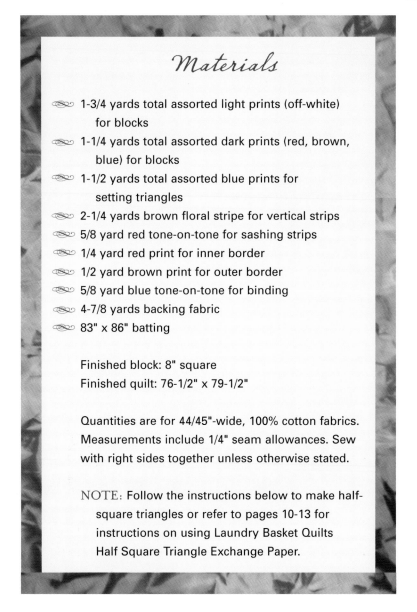

Materials

- 1-3/4 yards total assorted light prints (off-white) for blocks
- 1-1/4 yards total assorted dark prints (red, brown, blue) for blocks
- 1-1/2 yards total assorted blue prints for setting triangles
- 2-1/4 yards brown floral stripe for vertical strips
- 5/8 yard red tone-on-tone for sashing strips
- 1/4 yard red print for inner border
- 1/2 yard brown print for outer border
- 5/8 yard blue tone-on-tone for binding
- 4-7/8 yards backing fabric
- 83" x 86" batting

Finished block: 8" square
Finished quilt: 76-1/2" x 79-1/2"

Quantities are for 44/45"-wide, 100% cotton fabrics. Measurements include 1/4" seam allowances. Sew with right sides together unless otherwise stated.

NOTE: Follow the instructions below to make half-square triangles or refer to pages 10-13 for instructions on using Laundry Basket Quilts Half Square Triangle Exchange Paper.

Note: The quilt photographed was shortened to accommodate an antique bed frame. The block rows were trimmed 1" below the baskets in the bottom blocks. Instructions and measurements given here will result in the untrimmed quilt top shown in the Quilt Top Assembly Diagram on page 78.

Cut the Fabrics

From assorted light prints, cut:
8—2-1/2" squares
42—2-1/2" x 4-1/2" rectangles
52—2-7/8" squares
7—2-7/8" squares, cutting each in half diagonally for a total of 14 A triangles
1—3-3/8" square
11—4-7/8" squares, cutting each in half diagonally for a total of 22 B triangles

From assorted dark prints, cut:
25—2-1/2" squares
52—2-7/8" squares
19—2-7/8" squares, cutting each in half diagonally for a total of 38 A triangles
2—4-1/2" squares
9—4-7/8" squares, cutting each in half diagonally for a total of 18 B triangles

From assorted blue prints, cut:
12—12-1/2" squares, cutting each diagonally in an X for a total of 48 setting triangles

From brown floral stripe, cut:
4—7-1/4" x 80" vertical strips

From red tone-on-tone, cut:
12—1-1/2" x 42" sashing strips

From red print, cut:
4—1-1/2" x 42" inner border strips

From brown print, cut:
4—4" x 42" outer border strips

From blue tone-on-tone, cut:
8—2-1/2" x 42" binding strips

From backing, cut:
2—42" x 86" rectangles

Making Half-Square Triangles

1. With right sides together, layer a dark print 2-7/8" square with a light print 2-7/8" square. Draw a diagonal line across the wrong side of the light print square.

2. Sew 1/4" on both sides of the drawn line. Cut apart on the drawn line. Press seam toward the dark triangle. The half-square triangles should measure 2-1/2" square. Repeat Steps 1 and 2 to make a total of 104 half-square triangles. There will be one unused half-square triangle.

Make 104 half-square triangles

Assemble the Blocks

Note: The blocks are referred to by a letter and number. The letter refers to Row A, B, or C and the number (1-7) refers to the block's location from the top of the quilt. Each block uses a single light print fabric for the background pieces and for most of the half-square triangles. Refer to the photograph on page 79 for color placement ideas.

1. For Block A1, lay out four half-square triangles, one light print 2-1/2" square, one light print B triangle, two light print 2-1/2" x 4-1/2" rectangles, two dark print A triangles, and two dark print B triangles (one from each of two fabrics) as shown.

Block A1

2. Sew dark print B triangles together; press seam toward basket triangle. Sew half-square triangles together in pairs; add light print 2-1/2" square to one pair. Press seams in one direction. Sew these to B triangles for basket section. Sew dark print A triangles to two light print 2-1/2" x 4-1/2" rectangles for left and right side sections; press seams away from A. Sew side sections to basket section; press seams toward side sections. Add light print B triangle; press seam toward B.

Block A1
Assembly

3. For Blocks A2 and A7, lay out five half-square triangles, one light print B triangle, two light print 2-1/2" x 6-1/2" rectangles, two dark print A triangles (one from each of two fabrics), and two dark print B triangles as shown.

Blocks
A2 & A7

4. Sew dark print B triangles together; press seam toward basket triangle. Sew half-square triangles together in one pair and one row of three. Press seams in one direction. Sew these to B triangles for basket section. Sew dark print A triangles to two light print 2-1/2" x 4-1/2" rectangles for left and right side sections; press seams away from A. Sew side sections to basket section; press seams toward side sections. Add light print B triangle; press seam toward B.

Blocks
A2 & A7
Assembly

5. For Blocks A3, A6, B2, and C5 lay out six half-square triangles, two light print A triangles, one light print B triangle, two light print 2-1/2" x 4-1/2" rectangles, two dark print A triangles, and one dark print B triangle as shown.

Blocks
A3, A6,
B2 & C5

6. Sew half-square triangles and light print A triangles together in rows. Press seams in one direction, alternating the direction from row to row. Sew the rows together; press. Add the dark print B triangle to complete the basket section; press seam toward B. Sew dark print A triangles to two light print 2-1/2" x 4-1/2" rectangles for left and right side sections; press seams away from A. Sew side sections to basket section; press seams toward side sections. Add light print B triangle; press seam toward B.

Blocks
A3, A6,
B2 & C5
Assembly

7. For Block A4, lay out five half-square triangles, one light print 3-3/8" square, one light print B triangle, two light print 2-1/2" x 4-1/2" rectangles, six dark print A triangles (four of one fabric and two of a second fabric) as shown.

Block A4

8. Sew four matching dark print A triangles to the light print 3-3/8" square; press seams toward triangles. Sew half-square triangles together in one pair and one row of three. Press seams in one direction. Sew these to triangle/square for basket section. Sew dark print A triangles to two light print 2-1/2" x 4-1/2" rectangles for left and right side sections; press seams away from A.

Sew side sections to basket section; press seams toward side sections. Add light print B triangle; press seam toward B.

Block A4 Assembly

9. For Blocks A5 and B1, lay out four half-square triangles, one light print 2-1/2" square, one light print B triangle, two light print 2-1/2" x 4-1/2" rectangles, three dark print 2-1/2" squares (two of one fabric and one of a second fabric), and one dark print B triangle as shown.

Blocks A5 & B1

10. Sew half-square triangles and light and dark print squares together in rows. Press seams in one direction, alternating the direction from row to row. Sew two rows of three pieces together; press. Add a light print 2-1/2" x 4-1/2" rectangle to one end for the top section; press seam toward rectangle. Sew the dark and light B triangles together; press seam toward dark triangle. Sew the second rectangle to the half-square triangle/square; press seam toward rectangle. Add this to B triangles for bottom section; press seam toward B. Sew the top and bottom sections together; press.

Blocks A5 & B1 Assembly

11. For Blocks B3 and C4, lay out five half-square triangles, one light print B triangle, two light print 2-1/2" x 4-1/2" rectangles, four dark print 2-1/2" squares (three of one fabric and one of a second fabric), and two dark print A triangles as shown.

Blocks B3 & C4

12. Sew half-square triangles and dark print 2-1/2" squares together in rows. Press seams in one direction, alternating the direction from row to row. Sew the rows together for basket section; press. Sew dark print A triangles to two light print 2-1/2" x 4-1/2" rectangles for left and right side sections; press seams away from A. Sew side sections to basket section; press seams toward side sections. Add light print B triangle; press seam toward B.

Blocks B3 & C4 Assembly

13. For Blocks B4 and C1, lay out five half-square triangles, one light print B triangle, two light print 2-1/2" x 4-1/2" rectangles, one dark print 4-1/2" square, and two dark print A triangles as shown.

Blocks B4 & C1

14. Sew half-square triangles together in one pair and one row of three. Press seams in one direction. Sew these to the dark print 4-1/2" square for basket section. Sew dark print A triangles to two light print 2-1/2" x 4-1/2" rectangles for left and right side sections; press seams away from A. Sew side sections to basket section; press seams toward side sections. Add light print B triangle; press seam toward B.

Blocks B4 & C1 Assembly

15. For Blocks B5 and C3, lay out four half-square triangles, one light print 2-1/2" square, two light print A triangles, one light print B triangle, two light print 2-1/2" x 4-1/2" rectangles, one dark print 2-1/2" square, two dark print A triangles, and one dark print B triangle as shown.

Blocks B5 & C3

16. Sew two light print A triangles to adjacent sides of the dark print 2-1/2" square; press seams toward triangles. Sew these to dark print B triangle; press seam toward B. Sew half-square triangles together in pairs; add light print 2-1/2" square to one pair. Press seams in one direction. Sew these to dark B triangle for basket section. Sew dark print A triangles to two light print 2-1/2" x 4-1/2" rectangles for left and right side sections;

press seams away from A. Sew side sections to basket section; press seams toward side sections. Add light print B triangle; press seam toward B.

Blocks B5 & C3 Assembly

17. For Block B6, lay out four half-square triangles, one light print 2-1/2" square, one light print B triangle, two light print 2-1/2" x 4-1/2" rectangles, four dark print 2-1/2" squares (two from each of two fabrics), and two dark print A triangles as shown.

Block B6

18. Sew half-square triangles and light and dark print 2-1/2" squares together in rows. Press seams in one direction, alternating the direction from row to row. Sew the rows together for basket section; press. Sew dark print A triangles to two light print 2-1/2" x 4-1/2" rectangles for left and right side sections; press seams away from A. Sew side sections to basket section; press seams toward side sections. Add light print B triangle; press seam toward B.

Block B6 Assembly

19. For Blocks B7 and C2, lay out eight half-square triangles, one light print B triangle, two light

print 2-1/2" x 4-1/2" rectangles, and one dark print B triangle as shown.

Blocks B7 & C2

20. Sew half-square triangles together in rows. Press seams in one direction, alternating the direction from row to row. Sew two rows of three together; press. Add a light print 2-1/2" x 4-1/2" rectangle to one end for the top section; press seam toward rectangle. Sew the dark and light B triangles together; press seam toward dark triangle. Sew the second rectangle to the half-square triangle pair; press seam toward rectangle. Add this to B triangles for bottom section; press seam toward B. Sew the top and bottom sections together; press.

Blocks B7 & C2 Assembly

21. For Block C6, lay out four half-square triangles, two light print B triangles (one from each of two fabrics), two light print 2-1/2" x 4-1/2" rectangles, one dark print 2-1/2" square, two dark print A triangles, and one dark print B triangle as shown.

Block C6

22. Sew one light print B triangle to dark print B triangle; press seam toward dark triangle. Sew half-square triangles together in pairs; add dark print 2-1/2" square to one pair. Press seams in one direction. Sew these to B triangles for basket section. Sew dark print A triangles to two light print 2-1/2" x 4-1/2" rectangles for left and right side sections; press seams away from A. Sew side sections to basket section; press seams toward side sections. Add light print B triangle; press seam toward B.

Block C6 Assembly

23. For Block C7, lay out two light print 2-1/2" squares, two light print A triangles, one light print B triangle, two light print 2-1/2" x 4-1/2" rectangles, four dark print 2-1/2" squares, two dark print A triangles, and one dark print B triangle as shown.

Block C7

24. Sew light and dark print 2-1/2" squares and light print A triangles together in rows. Press seams in one direction, alternating the direction from row to row. Sew the rows together; press. Add the dark print B triangle to complete the basket section; press seam toward B. Sew dark print A triangles to two light print 2-1/2" x 4-1/2" rectangles for left and right side sections; press seams

away from A. Sew side sections to basket section; press seams toward side sections. Add light print B triangle; press seam toward B.

Block C7
Assembly

Assemble the Rows

1. Sew blue print setting triangles to opposite edges of each block to make a Block-Triangle unit as shown. Press seams toward the setting triangles. Repeat to make 21 Block-Triangle units.

Make 21
Block-Triangle units

2. Carefully matching seams, sew together seven Block-Triangle units in a row, arranging the blocks as desired. Press seams in one direction. Add a blue print setting triangle to each end. Repeat to make three rows.

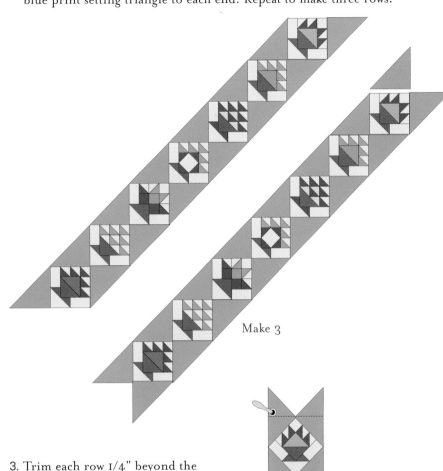

Make 3

3. Trim each row 1/4" beyond the points of the top and bottom blocks.

Album Basket Quilt

Assemble the Quilt Top

1. Sew together the red tone-on-tone 1-1/2" x 42" sashing strips in pairs to make six sashing strips. Join the red print 1-1/2" x 42" inner border strips and the brown print 4" x 42" outer border strips in pairs, making two inner border strips and two outer border strips.

2. Referring to Quilt Top Assembly Diagram, center and sew the red tone-on-tone 1-1/2"-wide sashing strips to the long edges of the rows. Press seams toward sashing strips. Trim sashing ends even with the rows.

3. Join the rows with brown floral stripe 7-1/4" x 80" strips. Add brown floral stripe strips to the left and right edges of quilt top. Press all seams toward sashing strips.

4. Add the red print 1-1/2"-wide inner border strips to the left and right edges and then the brown print 4"-wide outer border strips. Press seams toward the outer border.

Complete the Quilt

1. Sew together the 42" x 86" backing rectangles along one long edge, using a 1/2" seam allowance. Press the seam allowance open.

2. Layer quilt top, batting, and pieced backing.

3. Quilt as desired. The entire quilt top was stitched using an all-over large floral pattern.

4. Bind with blue tone-on-tone binding strips

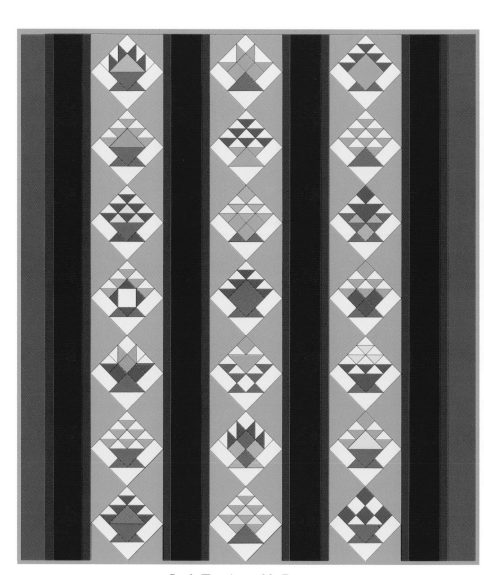

Quilt Top Assembly Diagram

Album Basket Quilt

Designed and pieced by Edyta Sitar for Laundry Basket Quilts

"Thanks for holding my hand."

Resources

Laundry Basket Quilts . . . . www.laundrybasketquilts.com

Moda Fabrics . . . . www.unitednotions.com

Julie Lillo - long arm quilter . . . . www.quiltedjewels.com

Aurifil™ Threads . . . . www.aurifil.com

Southern Exposure . . . . www.southernmoon.com

Landauer Corporation . . . . www.landauercorp.com

Visit your local quilt shop for Laundry Basket Quilts
Triangle Exchange Paper.

Darling Friend,
When distant lands divide us and you no more I'll
see just take a patch and needle and stitch a stitch
for me.